The
Mystery Fancier

Volume 5 Number 3
May/June 1981

The MYSTERY FANcier

Volume 5 Number 3
May/June 1981

TABLE OF CONTENTS

WILDSIDE PRESS

Mysteriously Speaking ...

This issue is one sheet (four pages) shorter than normal, the victim of a shortage of reviews and letters from you folks and my own obsession with getting back on schedule. Barring unforeseen foul-ups at the printer's or the post office, this issue, the May/June issue, should be in the mail by 11 May at the absolute latest. This gives me such a heady feeling that I'm going to try to get the July/August issue out sometime in June--provided, of course, that you folks send those articles, reviews, and letters on to me right away. There'll be no more short issues, if I can avoid it, but I really would like to get the next issue put together as soon as I've got fifty pages worth of material. And then, for the first time in what seems like ages, I can relax for a couple of months.

An item of interest to those of us who dream, openly or covertly, of one day writing a mystery (which is most of us, I'm sure)--Charles Scribner's has announced that it will be awarding The Charles Scribner's Crime Novel Award this year for the best first mystery submitted to it for publication-- $7,500 altogether, $5,000 of which will be an advance against royalties, the rest will be a cash prize. The publicity blurb:

" ... Books eligible for the Scribner Crime Novel Award should be by an American author or a permanent U.S. resident and may include novels of classic detection, historical re- constructions, fictionalized "true crime," espionage, police procedurals and private-eye stories. The supernatural in any form as well as pastiche and parody, whether of Sherlock Holmes or any other established character in fiction, will be excluded.

"Entries ... should be submitted to Charles Scribner's Sons, 597 Fifth Avenue, New York, New York 10017, and must be clearly marked as being submitted for ... the ... prize. They must be received by September 30, 1981. Submissions must be in the form of completed manuscripts. Manuscripts must be typed, double spaced, one side only of regular typewriter paper (8½ x 11) and should include a self-addressed manila envelope with return postage.

"Winners will be announced early in 1982. In addition to publishing the prize [novel], the publishers reserve the right to offer publication on the usual terms for any of the other manuscripts submitted."

1

A CHINESE DETECTIVE IN SAN FRANCISCO

By E.F. Bleiler

The San Francisco Chinatown, in its heyday around the turn of the century, was undoubtedly the most important Chinese settlement in the New World. This was obvious even to those who were not Chinese. Tourists came great distances to gape through it; photographers like Arnold Genthe took pictures that are among the classical documents of American historical photography; and literary men used it as a source for colorful background material.

One of the San Francisco litterateurs who worked this vein of Oriental culture was Chester Bailey Fernald, a local newspaperman. He wrote several stories that were set in Chinatown, one of which, "The Cat and the Cherub," served as the source for a fairly popular play. Of more specialized interest, however, is the fact that a traditional Chinese detective story lies concealed within one of Fernald's dialect pieces.

This story is "Chan Tow the Highrob," which appears in the book *The Cat and the Cherub and Other Stories* (New York: Century, 1896) and may have appeared in periodical form a year or two earlier. It is presented as a dialogue between two persons, a journalist named Gordon, and his chinese friend and informant, Fuey Fong. The story is buried in a heavy Chinese dialect, with many misdirections and interruptions and a strong note of ethnic humor. When Fuey Fong, for example, speculates why, as an Oriental, he is not allowed to attend the Christian Endeavor Society, the name comes out as the "Christingin Indevil Shoshiety." The story that Fuey Fong tells is garbled both in language and in concept, but here is what might be called a clear summary:

"Chan To the Highwayman"

This is the story of the disappearance of the wealthy merchant Jan Han Sun.

The merchant Jan Han Sun travelled to the province of Kansu and spent several months there conducting his business. When he had amassed a considerable amount of money, he decided to return to his home in the Prefecture of Tung-Ren. He set out on foot, carrying his wealth with him in the form of gold and silver.

It was a long journey. When he came to his home town, he first paid a ceremonial visit to his parents-in-law, since his own parents were dead, and this was the correct thing to do. He left their house, saying that he was going to his own home, and apparently disappeared along the way. Nothing more was seen of him.

Jan's wife, when she heard that he had arrived in town, seemed convinced that something had happened to him and placed an accusation against her own parents, claiming that they must have murdered Jan for his gold and silver. The local magistrate arrested the parents, investigated the accusation, but could discover nothing. The parents seemed obviously innocent and were released. Jan's wife thereupon appealed to the higher authorities in the Prefecture, who informed the district magistrate that if he did not solve the case within six months,

2

he would be degraded and would lose his position.

This put the magistrate in a difficult situation, since he had conscientiously investigated the case and had discovered nothing. If he were reduced a grade in rank, he might never hold another official post, for competition for appointments was severe. The thought occurred to him that he might gather information from the local criminal population. He thereupon disguised himself as a diviner (which occupation was considered low), and wandered the roads and frequented the thieves' dens, trying to draw out information about the suspected crime. But he had no success at all.

Time passed, and the end of the six month period was drawing near. As he was wandering down one of the roads outside his town one night, in desperation he stopped and prayed to his ancestors and to the gods, begging for help. As if in answer to his prayer, he saw a flickering light, not too far away. He approached it and found a small house. The old woman who owned the house told him that he could have shelter, but that her son was Chan To the Highwayman, and that Chan To, when he returned, might object to his presence.

When Chan To arrived, he turned out to be quite hospitable, and he and the magistrate soon became friendly and exchanged stories. As they sat drinking hot wine together, the magistrate commented on the mysterious disappearance of the merchant Jan, which had baffled the authorities.

"It is a great mystery," said the disguised mandarin, "and I doubt if anyone will ever know what happened."

"Oh, no. Not at all," said Chan To. "It's no mystery. I know all about it. In fact, I saw it." He then proceeded to tell this story to the magistrate. Chan had been in Kansu Province, and he had heard of Jan's wealth. He decided to rob Jan, but circumstances were always against him. When Jan set out on the road, Chan followed close behind him, but Jan carefully remained in company and even went to the extent of sitting on his possessions when he ate at inns. "I have never seen such a suspicious man," said Chan To.

Chan stayed on the merchant's trail all the way back from Kansu and finally decided to burglarize Jan's house when Jan was sleeping. He followed Jan to his parents-in-law's, and then to Jan's own house. When Jan went in, Chan swiftly climbed up on the roof and worked the tiles aside, so that he could see into the room below. He planned to descend when everyone was asleep.

"But do you know what was strange?" said Chan To to the magistrate. "His wife was not expecting him, and was surprised to see him, yet the table was set for two."

Jan could not help but notice this, too, and asked his wife about it. She coyly replied that when Jan was away she loved him so much that she pretended he was present. This pleased old Jan greatly, and he began to drink heavily and soon fell into a drunken stupor.

Jan's wife tried to arouse him several times, but when she saw that he would not awaken, she went over to the wall, removed clothing from a cupboard, and knocked on the wall. A door in the back of the cupboard opened, and a handsome young man came in from the house next door. He was obviously Mrs. Jan's lover. She urged the young man to kill Jan, so that they could get married, but the young man, who seemed timid, was unwilling, and Mrs. Jan had to scream at him and tongue-lash him into doing the deed. Finally, he stabbed Jan. The murderous pair then took up a floor slab and buried the corpse beneath it.

"I left immediately," said Chan To, "for I'm an honest highwayman, not a killer, and I didn't want to be entangled in a murder."

The magistrate realized that his quest was over. The next morning he returned to his yamen, removed his disguise, and had his constables bring in all the parties concerned. He charged Jan's wife and her lover with murder. The presence of the corpse where Chan To said it would be made denials impossible, and both confessed. While the lover was cowardly and tearful, Mrs. Jan, when sentenced to be beheaded, was defiant, and loudly proclaimed that she did not mind dying, as long as she was with her lover.

The magistrate then asked Chan To, whom the constables had brought in as a witness, if he recognized him. Chan To did not, whereupon the magistrate revealed himself as the diviner. Chan To swore to reform his way of life, and he became a valued assistant to the magistrate.

As can be seen, "The Story of Chan To" corresponds closely to the pattern revealed in other Chinese detective stories, particularly the *Dee Goong An*, as translated by van Gulik. The narrative is chronological in organization. The magistrate ventures in disguise to obtain information. He is aided by minimal divine assistance. The criminal turns out to be a lustful woman, who is the prime mover, while a weak lover lives next door on the other side of a secret panel. The woman dies defiantly. And the magistrate enlists the basically good-hearted highwayman as his assistant.

The question arises where Fernald obtained this traditional Chinese detective story. Did one of his Chinese friends read in one of the printed collections of detective stories and narrate it to him? Is it the plot of a Chinese play performed in the San Francisco Chinatown? Is it a folktale? We do not know, although the story would seem to be literary in origin, rather than completely oral. The names, for example, are not in Cantonese form (*ren* being impossible), but Mandarin.

As to the anonymous magistrate-detective, I wish that we knew his name. While neither Dee nor Bao had an assistant named Chan To in the adventures I have read, it is quite possible that Chan To may appear in other stories. Or the mandarin may have been one of the many other great detectives in Chinese history. Perhaps some Sinologist can tell us.

REVIEW ARTICLE

THE SKENE MELVIN BIBLIOGRAPHY OF CRITICAL WRITING

By Walter Albert

> Details, details, details! The most insig-
> nificant, the most unobtrusive among them
> are often the most evocative, characteristic
> and even decisive. Exact details, an artful
> little nothing, make art.
>
> —Max Ophuls

David and Ann Skene Melvin, compilers. *Crime, Detective, Espionage, Mystery and Thriller Fiction & Film: A Comprehensive Bibliography of Critical Writing Through 1979.*
Westport, Connecticut: Greenwood Press, 1980, 368 pp.,
$29.95.

The compilation of bibliographies is one of the most te-
dious and thankless of researchers' tasks. I take it to be
the job of the bibliographer to make information available in
as economical, straightforward, and accurate manner as possible. It is an open-ended work since no bibliography is ever
complete, and the details are displayed in such a fashion that
the bibliographer's errors in judgment and fact are quickly
apparent to everyone except, perhaps, the poor bibliographer
himself, whose tunnel vision often blinds him to the faulty
detail which he will later find--after it has been pointed out
to him--he has incorrectly transcribed from his notes or taken,
if he has not had access to the primary material, from an in-
accurate source.

I can, then, recognize that the Skene Melvins' bibliography
involved an enormous amount of work, even as I regretfully
must admit that I find them to have seriously compromised the
usefulness of their book in at least two areas: comprehensive-
ness of coverage, and precision and economy in the presentation.

This second reservation may be seen by some as not seriously damaging to the text. It is essentially a question of
style, but in a medium as concise as a bibliography the style
is inevitably wedded to the content. Thus, I do not consider
it a trivial matter and I think that if I begin my discussion
with an examination of the work's stylistic aberrations the
deficiencies in style can be more easily understood as a func-
tion of deficiencies in concept and content.

In their directions on "how to use the bibliography," the
Skene Melvins state that the form of entry is "primarily that
of the Library of Congress." What they do not appear to take
into account is that the Library of Congress listing is a
cataloguing system, not a bibliographic one. The bibliographic
entry is more concise and the form of notation used is quite
different. It is, of course, standard bibliographic practice
to follow the form suggested by the MLA Style Sheet and the
University of Chicago *Manual of Style*, with the choice of detail being made on the basis of clarity and consistency.

A typical book entry in Skene Melvin appears as follows:

6. Adams, Elsie Bonita (1932-   ). *Israel Zangwill*. N.Y.: Twayne;
   1971. 177p. (Twayne's English Authors series no. 121).

The information is clearly given but there are at least four
deviations from standard bibliographic style: the inclusion
of the author's dates, the use of a semi-colon instead of a
comma after the publisher, the use of "p." as an abbreviation
for pages, and the displacement of series data from its usual
position after the title. One can observe that the semi-colon
is syntactically bizarre, that "p." is used in cataloguing
entries for "pp." and the furnishing of dates is not consis-
tent; it is, rather, the exception and apparently occurs only
where the information was taken from a Library of Congress
listing. I also find that bibliographies that are most useful
to me indicate the presence--or absence--of a bibliography
and/or index, and it is the kind of information one would have
expected if the source had been consulted for verification of
data and format.

The entries for articles are also unusual and are an example of the lack of economy which I find most troubling in
the stylistic variants adopted by the Skene Melvins.

7. . . . "Israel Zangwill; an annotated bibliography of writings
about him." IN *English Literature in Transition; 1880-1920.* v.13
(1970) pp. 203-209.

The authors explain in their introduction that when there is
more than one item by an author, repetition is shown by ellipsis (...). The common meaning taken for an ellipsis is that
it is "the omission of one or more words that can be obviously
understood," or "a leap or sudden passage . . . from one topic
to another." (The ellipsis is mine, not the authors'.) Suc-
cessive author entries in bibliographies are usually indicated
not by an ellipsis but by a bar followed by a period, as in
_____. An ellipsis is an omission, and I think it a fairly
audacious semantic leap to call the sign used as a substitution
for a name an ellipsis.

The use of "IN" to show that an entry can be found in a
journal is not used in any bibliography I know of; it is commonly used to show that an article is included in an anthology.
It is certainly superfluous here. For journal titles in comprehensive bibliographies, a master list of acronyms is normally established, a convenient shorthand that conserves precious
space. The "v." would be unnecessary since the first number
after the journal name is understood to be the volume; and,
since the final numbers are universally taken to indicate the
pagination, the use of "pp." is not necessary. Thus, the
entry, in standard bibliographic notation, would read as
follows:

7. _____. "Israel Zangwill: An Annotated Bibliography of Writings
About Him." ELT 13:203-209.

The entries for joint author titles are even less concise
and economical than the entries I have just described.

24. Allen, Richard Stanley. (jnt. comp.) *Detective Fiction: crime
and compromise.* (Ed. by Dick Allen and David Chacko. N.Y.: Harcourt Brace Jovanovich; 1974. xiv, 481p.

This is undoubtedly the quirkiest of the formats. All the
"jnt. comp." volumes have a main entry under the first listed
compiler and separate entries for the other compiler or compilers, identified by an asterisk in the alphabetical listing
and cross referenced in this way:

* Chacko, David (jnt. ed.). SEE Allen, R.S. (jnt. ed.).

One can note that "jnt. comp." has become "jnt. ed.," and I
see no rational explanation for this. (Are the authors com-

pilers or editors? Surely, there is a difference, and it could have been determined.) What is curious is that the Chacko reference is to Allen, R.S. (jnt. ed.), when Allen is clearly listed alphabetically as the "jnt. comp." Furthermore, in the main entry, it is Allen, Dick who is "jnt. ed." Does Richard prefer to be called Dick by his friends and are the Skene Melvins subtly giving us some private information? In any event, use of standard bibliographic style would have produced this simpler, more concise entry:

Allen, Richard Stanley (or Dick and David Chacko, eds. *Detective Fiction: Crime and Compromise.* NY: Harcourt Brace Jovanovich, 1974. xiv+481 pp.

If, in matters of detail, the bibliography is erratic and unclear, in concept it is not comprehensive in its coverage of critical writing or the history of detective and mystery fiction.

In their defensive introduction, the authors offer a brief history of the field which they see as having begun with Poe. This historical cropping is curious in light of the fact that, although they exclude all material earlier than Poe's and all macabre/fantasy/ghosts/supernatural/gothis/sci-fi material, they include "shockers" without apparently realizing that the shocker has a history pre-dating 1841 and should open up consideration of the penny dreadful and the gothic novel. This does seem to indicate a fairly substantial unfamiliarity with literary history and means, in addition, that nothing can presumably be done with such a major historical figure as Vidocq (although his *Mémoires* of 1828 are included), or with Julian Symons' contention that "the characteristic note of crime fiction is first struck in *Caleb Williams*, by William Godwin, which appeared in 1794." Moreover, in spite of their resolve, the mystery/science fiction breach is repaired by entries on Asimov's *Caves of Steel*, the supernatural prohibition is contradicted by material on the psychic detective, and the ban on pre01841 material is not only lifted for Vidocq but also for E.T.A. Hoffman (1776-1822). Not an overwhelming number of exceptions, but leaks in the dam which expose the faults in the basic premises.

There is, however, a further area of exclusion which is even more damaging. One of the points made with some force in the introduction in defense of the genre is that traditional critical distinctions between literature (which is worth "critical attention") and "fiction" (intended for mass consumption and definitely not literature) are impossible to maintain with any rigor. An unexceptionable stand, I think, and one that I agree with completely. Yet still anothet stereotype is resurrected to establish the basis on which the respectability of sources is determined. Thus, although the editors believe that a novel whose subject is crime does not "necessarily mean that it is second-rate," they speak of the "uncritical adulation of the fanzine" and exclude such material unless it is referred to in a "respectable" source. This uninformed decision also extends to the exclusion of material from *The Armchair Detective*, which most people consider the **major** critical journal in **the** field. This decision was not, we are told, made on the bias of fanzine bias but rather because the bibliographers felt that to have, as they put it, "indexed" TAD would have "stretched the bibliography beyond

8

manageable proportions." If one prepared a bibliography of Victorian material without including *Victorian Studies,* I rather imagine that no reputable scholar would consider the undertaking comprehensive or of great usefulness. The point is that including TAD references would not provide an index to TAD but simply incorporate that material from the magazine which one normally enters in a bibliography. If, as I believe it is, the purpose of a comprehensive bibliography is to provide in one place a record of the significant critical contributions to a field, then this bibliography is gravely deficient. If the bibliography, as they conceived and structured it, would not allow for the inclusion of a substantial body of important material, then the concept should have been re-examined and the structure of the work re-thought.

In planning the bibliography, the editors had decided that the "most useful arrangement with the least duplication was to list the material [alphabetically] and to provide both a title and a subject index." Indexes are necessary elements in reference texts, and the editors are to be commended for providing them. However, much of the subject index is, in fact, an author index, and if the material had been arranged by subject rather than by author in the body of the work, the 90-page subject index could have been substantially eliminated. I find this not an elimination of "duplication" but rather a clear case of contributing to it. And I might also note that each entry in the index is double-spaced, an advantage is material is going to be set in type, but a profligate use of space that might be more usefully filled if length, as it obviously was, is a matter of concern.

There is a curious relationship between the inefficient journal and book entries and the inefficient organization of the components. On the one hand, there is the expressed desire to be "comprehensive" which I believe I have shown is not true, and, on the other hand, the recording of data in a form in which neither economy nor clarity is a prime consideration.

There is a further point to be made about the entries. The authors call this an "international" bibliography, and it is true that material from several languages is provided. However, to speak only of the French, with which I am familiar, there is no material from the leading journal *Enigmatika* or from any of the several other magazines in which important articles have been appearing since the mid-seventies. There is also the question of the nature of the foreign-language material. While many of the users of the bibliography may be able to read the German, Italian or French entries, the Japanese, Dutch, Scandinavian and Russian entries, none of which is translated, often give no clue as to the nature of the content. I assume that the bibliographers are not proficient in all of the languages they cited. If they are, I compliment them and respectfully request that, in a future edition, they provide translations of the titles. If they are not, and were advised by someone proficient in that (those) language(s), I would appreciate it if they would make available to me--and to other readers--the information which was given to them and which justified the inclusion of the entry.

This justification is another area of the bibliography I should like to address. My idea of a bibliography is that the material should either be partially or largely self-explanatory and if the justification is not self-evident--as

in "Traffic in Souls" and "Blood Marks in the Sylvan Glades,"
to cite only two of many examples--a brief statement clarify-
ing the entry for the reader is in order. Bibliographies
should not in themselves present mysteries for the reader to
solve. A common failing in this respect is in citing books
as if the whole volume were the reference when only passages
in it are surely relevant. I will list a few of the more
flagrant examples: 537. *Pages from the Goncourt Journal*; 547.
Violence in Modern Literature; 554. *The Long Weekend: A Social
History of Great Britain (1918-1939)*; and 529. *Happy Rural
Seat: The English Country House and the Literary Imagination.*
    This tendency to address large topics when only some of
the material is relevant is also evident in the attention
given to comics. I agree with the authors that there is much
material in comic books and comic strips that would interest
scholars and readers in the field. However, the inclusions--
with no page or subject references--of Les Daniel's *Comix,*
Maurice Horn's *Women in the Comics,* Don Thompson and Richard
Lupoff's *The Comic-book Book, The World Encyclopedia of Comics*
and Waugh's *The Comics* are hardly the kinds of references that
will be helpful to a researcher.
    There is another kind of entry whose validity I question.
To my knowledge, a bibliography is the record of published
material in a field. Unlike any other bibliography with which
I am familiar, this text also records works-in-progress, works
announced by publishers but with no later record of actual
publication, speeches and, in one instance, an unpublished
five page article (item 1070). There are also bibliographic
references which the authors solemnly note they have not been
able to verify. One of these supposedly unverifiable sources
is James Sandoe's *The Hardboiled Dick: A Personal Checklist,*
which I have seen offered for sale by dealers and used as a
reference by scholars who appear to have worked from the
material; in short, a standard source whose existence no one
has ever questioned. The authors add that "according to Nolan
... this item was reprinted in TAD v. 1: no. 2 (January 1968)."
Surely this information about TAD would not have been difficult to verify. If the skene Melvins did not have direct
access to a run to TAD, a note to publisher Allen Hubin would
have quickly confirmed the reprint and undoubtedly also confirmed the "phantom" pamphlet's existence.
    This last point raises an intriguing issue. Although the
authors give their "thanks and appreciation to correspondents
around the world," they do not name a single one. Whatever
the nature of their correspondence, it was not the kind in
which one verifies references, points out that "unverified"
item no. 1568 can be found in the National Union Catalogue of
pre-1965 imprints on page 594 in volume 668, or understands
that the version of Raymond Chandler's "The Simple Art of
Murder" reprinted in *Crime in Good Company* (Constable, 1959)
and described in Skene Melvin entry 254, is, in fact, the
version described in entry 253. In addition, if the bibliography is complete up to 1979, it should have recorded in item
254 the further appearance of the essay as an introduction to
the 1971 anthology *The Midnight Raymond Chandler.*
    Fortunately, this bibliographic source is not the only one
available to the reader. Robert Briney, in *The Mystery Story*
(Publishers Inc., 1976), edited by John Ball, published a
lengthy essay on secondary material which is a well-annotated

guide to basic references; *The Armchair Detective* publishes annually--as it has been doing since 1972--an international bibliography of secondary sources compiled and annotated by this reviewer; the Barzun-Taylor *Catalogue of Crime* (Scribners, 1971) has excellent coverage of the pre-1970 period; and Jon L. Breen (if I may be excused for including work-in-progress) is publishing a selective bibliography of secondary sources which is promised for the spring by Scarecrow Press.

This bibliography was long overdue; what is unfortunate is that the editors failed to conceive properly the scope of their project, were both careless and uninformative in the crucial matter of detail, and have prematurely published a text that with more careful and intelligent editing might well have been both comprehensive and indispensable. It is, with all of its faults, a text that many people will find useful, but until a thoroughly revised and corrected text is published, serious researchers will find themselves obliged to go to other sources for basic information this bibliography fails to provide.

ROGUES FOR THE NEW CENTURY

By Fred Dueren

A review of *Queen's Quorum* turns up many legendary titles
that a mystery fan seldom has a chance to see. Now Dover has
reprinted Grant Allen's *An African Millionaire* (1897), making
generally available for the first time one of crime fictions
all-time classics. For *An African Millionaire* holds up remarkably well. It is a bit naive in portions of the plot, but
the characters come alive and the suspense of the final chapter is a lesson in crime writing.

However, this is not a review of *An African Millionaire*,
but rather a comparison of it with another novel written a
decade later--*Get-Rich-Quick Wallingford* (1908), by George
Randolph Chester. The books have a common interest in swindler and businessmen. The individual stories comprising *An
African Millionaire* were originally printed in *The Straind*
magazine in 1896-1897. *An African Millionaire* is a British
work; *Get-Rich-Quick Wallingford* is distinctly American.

An African Millionaire is made up of twelve episodes,
nine of which involve intricate schemes and swindles in which
the notorious Colonel Clay outwits Sir Charles Vandrift. The
book has a unique idea in that all of Colonel Clay's crimes
are perpetrated against the same man. Vandrift made his fortune in African diamonds, then settled in England. He keeps
his hand in various business but seemse to spend most of his
time travelling and enjoying the life of the idle rich. The
stories are told by Seymour Wentworth, Vandrift's brother-in-
law and secretary. Colonel Clay is a notorious swindler,
known by the police of all Europe, but able to completely
evade them and keep his true identity a secret.

Get-Rich-Quick Wallingford is made up of twenty-eight
chapters, but only six major schemes. J. Rufus Wallingford is
an impressive adventurer. He crosses the country bilking one
and all of their savings and livelihood by selling them watered
stock, convincing them they'll make a fortune by sticking with
him. In attendance are his wife Fanny, a somewhat unwilling
accomplice, and cohort Blackie Daw, a less-successful con-man.

These are only superficial differences, however. Of more
interest is a comparison of the main characters' personalities
and an examination of the books' messages for their time.
Each is a strong tract against the excesses and power of money.

Wallingford is portrayed again and again as a grifter, a
con-man. His only interest is his own well-being. He "never
take[s] a chance" and boasts that he always has the law on his
side. He will delude an entire town into believing in his
schemes, and then he'll systematically take every penny he
can extract--from the poor as well as the rich. Two intro-
ductory items in the book set the atmosphere that business is
not a fully honorable profession. First is the subtitle: "A
cheerful account of the rise and fall of an American Business
Buccaneer." The phrase "American Business Buccaneer" strongly
ties the idea of piracy and taking what does not rightly be-
long to one, with the world of everyday business.

The second item is the dedication: "To the live businessmen of America--those who have been 'stung' and those who have
yet to undergo that painful experience--this little tale is

sympathetically dedicated." There is a taint on any business-
man that he is engaged in questionable activities, bound to be
"stung" by his fellow entrepreneurs, and deserving of sympathy
for merely being a member of that group.

Despite the light tone of the dedication and subtitle,
several times Wallingford is portrayed in the worst possible
light. His attitude is, "I need money and must have it." But
that need is for his own selfish wants, for the ability to eat
thr-e-hour meals and bedazzle others with his lavish spending.
Wallingford is all the more despicable because he is benevolent
and free-spending only so long as it furthers his plans to get
money from others. Once they are on to his game, and free-
spending will no longer increase his income, Wallingford's
spending is only for his own pleasure.

Sir Charles in *An African Millionaire* is no more admirable,
and he has the added irritant of assuming he is smarter and
better than others. Wallingford is calculating and knows he
is running a game, but Vandrift looks on everything as business. He deludes himself about his honor and integrity. He
has no compunction or second thought about cheating a poor
person out of the true value of diamonds. Vandrift has little
conscience and an overwhelming ego that does him in again and
again. Both men look on their activities as acceptable behavior. Let the buyer beware. If they can outsmart the suck-
er, so much the better. For each, money is their god and
business the proper form of worship.

Wallingford is most interesting in that he is comparable
to Colonel Clay and to a lesser extent to Vandrift. He is a
thief, a swindler, a master schemer like Clay. Both spend
months setting up plans and creating a character and situation
to bilk their victims. Both men use their wives to further
their plans. Clay's wife plays an active part, changing dis-
guises with him, helping him set up the pigeon one way or another. Fanny Wallingford, however, is more of a passive prop,
a decoration that Wallingford uses to impress his victims
with his social eminence and air of breeding. (An interesting
contrast of the wives is in their attitude toward their hus-
bands' activities. Clay's wife--most commonly referred to as
White Heather--not only helps him, but seems to spur him on.
We get the impression she would harrass Vandrift even if her
husband didn't. But Fanny is always against Wallingford's
schemes. She is aware of his ulterior purposes, usually, and
would prefer that he go into an honest business, settle down
in one town. At one point she asks him, "Have you noticed
another thing? Our money never does us any good.")

The basic hook that both men use to land their fish is
greed. Wallingford's usual procedure is to move into town,
establish credit, and set up a business that promises to make
thousands for the co-entrepreneurs he recruits. When he explains how they'll make a fortune from "the simple trick of
watering stock," they are immensely pleased. "They had heard
of such things as being vague and mysterious operations in the
realms of finance and had condemned them, taking their tone
from the columns of editorials they had read upon such prac-
tices; but now that they were themselves to reap the fruits of
it, they looked through different spectacles."

In a voice that "was the voice of Wall Street, of the
Government Mint, of the very soul and spirit of all financial
wisdom," he makes the anticipated profits so attractive that

in their rush to be a part of his business, townspeople throw
themselves and their money at him. All for the lure of astro-
nomical returns. Clay, likewise, plays continually on Vandrift's greed. It may involve purchasing diamonds far below
value, or buying a Tyrolean castle because it is more suitable
to Vandrift's idea of his station in life, or a chance to make
(or save) money on the stock exchange. It is always Vandrift's
desire that allows Clay to get the best of him. Clay speaking
to Vandrift says, "*You* are a capitalist and a millionaire. In
your large way you prey upon society. *You* deal in Corners,
Options, Concessions, Syndicates. You drain the world dry of
its blood and its money. You possess, like the mosquito, a
beautiful instrument of suction--Founders' Shares--with which
you absorb the surplus wealth of the community. In *my* smaller
way, again, *I* relieve you in turn of a portion of the plunder."
     Another variation of the use of greed is Clay's entrapment
of Wentworth (Vandrift's secretary) through his own greed.
During one of Clay's games, Wentworth acts as an intermediary.
For a proposed ten-percent commission of the difference, Wentworth offers to "negotiate" a better deal for Clay. Clay
agrees to a commission but pays by check, rather than cash as
agreed upon, and then uses the cancelled check to prevent ex-
posure if Wentworth ever identifies him during a scam.
     Both Clay and Wallingford enjoy the con for its own sake.
At their one face-to-face confrontation, Vandrift asks why
Clay is telling him certain things. Clay's reply is, "Because
I *love* the game ... and also because the more prepared you are
beforehand, the greater the credit and amusement there is in
besting you." (Wentworth also becomes intoxicated with the
contest. "Colonel Clay had stopped away for some months, it
is true, and for my own part, I will confess, since it wasn't
my place to pay the piper, I rather missed the wonted excite-
ment than otherwise.")
     Wallingford also loves the thrill of the chase. He de-
mands and enjoys money and the luxury and carelessness it can
buy. But just as important is the means of obtaining it. "So
ong as other people had money, the intricacies of finance were
only a pleasant recreation to him." But an odd thing happens
to Wallingford as the book develops. At the beginning he is a
carefree grafter, no more, no less. He appears in a new town
with only his fancy clothes, his debonair attitude, and "less
than one hundred dollars he carried in his pocket, nor had Mr.
Wallingford the slightest idea of where he was to get more.
This latter circumstance did not distress him, however; he
knew that there was still plenty of money in the world and
that none of it was soldered on." For each of his deals he
manages to put aside a tidy sum, until he amasses half a
million dollars. The idea then takes hold of being a true
millionaire, of having a reputation as a great financier, of
living with the richest of the country. "Heretofore his
operations had been on such a small scale that they could be
called 'common grafting,' but now, with a larger scope, they
would be termed 'shrewd financiering.' It was entirely a matter of proportion." When his scheme fails, he loses his half
million and is crushed and embittered. The man responsible
for his downfall he indignantly calls "a thief and a grafter!"
A bitter pill indeed. With the acquisition of wealth, Wallingford seems to have lost his joy in the game.
     Get-Rich-Quick Wallingford often reflects that the only

difference between grifters and financiers is the size of their
operations. Vandrift and Wallingford both make it a point to
stay within the law. They may be censured morally for their
actions, but not legally. Vandrift apparently has enough money
that he could retire with ease. But every pound that Colonel
Clay extracts from him smarts sharply. As Clay takes more and
more, Vandrift becomes more paranoid and greedy.

At the beginning of *An African Millionaire*, Vandrift is a
likeable fellow, foolish, perhaps, in his greed, but not ob-
jectionable. As the book progresses, he turns suspicious and
sour. More and more often he calls Wentworth a fool and openly
shows that he has little regard for Wentworth or his feelings.
(Likewise, Wentworth becomes more aware of Vandrift's true
personality and has increasingly less respect for him.) In
addition to Wentworth's lowering opinion of Vandrift, Colonel
Clay's letters specifically point out the reprehensible behavior of Sir Charles that allowed Clay to take advantage of
him.

Get-Rich-Quick Wallingford does not have a specific narra-
tor as *An African Millionaire* does, but Wallingford's behavior
also becomes noticeably more reprehensible as the book progresses. One of his all-time low points is the episode of the
Pneumatic Sales Recorder Company, in which he gets a competi-
tor drunk and then drugs him to be sure he does not spoil the
scheme that Wallingford is working on. After Maylie (the
conspirator-competitor) passes out, Wallingford calmly searches
his pockets and papers for information and verification of his
suspicions. These are actions we would expect from any common
thief. Or from a private eye looking for clues in his efforts
to uphold a moral code and restore order to a chaotic world.
Wallingford's use of them is purely for his own ends and personal profit. Capable of performing these deeds, it is not
surprising that Wallingford would ask, "*Is* a dollar honest?"

Both Wallingford and Vandrift are self-centered men. Their
concern for money is simply gratification of their own wants
and needs. In spite of their seeming success and outward
likeability, they are selfish, piggish men. Both are loners,
keeping their plans and ideas about their money to themselves.
Vandrift does not confide in Wentworth (thereby losing money
and inadvertantly saving Wentworth's) and Wallingford never
tells his wife or Blackie Daw exactly how he will turn a deed
to his advantage.

If we are to find a moral in the books, it is probably
best to draw from *Get-Rich-Quick Wallingford*. The following
statement is made to Wallingford but applies equally well to
Vandrift: "You're not an individual criminal at all. You're
only the logical development of the American tendency to 'get
there' no matter how." The books have held up well through
the years, even if they seem a bit simple at times, and some
of the deceptions are somewhat transparent. As crime stories,
they were a popular form of entertainment. As tracts against
the evils of greed and business they gently prod the conscience.

THE FATHERS AND SONS OF JOHN LE CARRE*

BY HARRY D. DAWSON

A commonplace motif in much of the spy fiction of our time has been the portrayal of spy and spy-master in terms of father-and-son relationships. At one extreme, such relationships are founded on deep mutual trust, as with Fleming's James Bond and "M" and with Donald Hamilton's Matt Helm and "Mac." In contrast, Len Deighton's anonymous spy, though Dawlish's top agent and protegé, is acutely aware of his boss's diabolism and constantly fears becoming a pawn in one of the spy-master's Machiavellian plots. In these and similar examples, the father-son motif is little more than a convention of the genre, though one which allows for a good deal of flexibility in character development. In the George Smiley novels of John le Carré, however, the father-son relationship is allowed to grow into a complex metaphor of generational betrayal and dynastic usurpation suggestive of the serious themes underlying le Carré's work. His ability to enrich the conventions of a popular genre is a significant factor in a growing body of evidence that le Carré is one of the best British novelists writing today.

Smiley's entry into the Secret Service (the "Circus" in the novels) begins the complex web of father-son relationships with which le Carré works. Smiley is recruited from Oxford by his tudor, Jebedee, for a mysterious organization run by a group of unconventional Oxbridge intellectuals and referred to by "Steed-Asprey, who seemed to be Chairman ... as the Secret Service." [*Call for the Dead*] When the series opens, however, the men of this generation have all departed. The agency is dominated by the opportunistic bureaucrat Maston, who wears "the cloak for his masters, ... preserving the dagger for his servants," a man Steed-Asprey had called "the Head Eunuch." [*Call for the Dead*] During Maston's administration, Smiley must suffer the role of despised step-child; Maston, however, is eventually replaced by the enigmatic but brilliant "Control," who recognizes Smiley's unique gifts as a super-spy and makes him his protegé. Smiley becomes the conscience of the agency, but before he can inherit the Circus patrimony, another usurper must be deposed. Percy Alleline, the incompetent politician of *Tinker, Tailor, Soldier, Spy* (1974), assumes control of the service after Control's death and chooses as his heir-apparent Bill Haydon, whom Smiley comes out of retirement to expose as a Soviet agent. This revelation, of course, brings down the Alleline regime, and Smiley assumes his rightful place as "lord" of his Secret Service domain.

Basic to the entire series is the role of Peter Guillam, Smiley's younger counterpart, errand boy, and chief aide, "smoother, but not glossy -rather a boyish figure, although ... he wasn't less than forty." [*The Spy Who Came in from the Cold*] Guillam chauffeurs Smiley around in a sports car and shares in the fluctuations of Smiley's fortunes within the Service: "When Alleline's crowd took over he was shoved out to grass in Brixton--he supposed because he had the wrong connections, among them Smiley." [*Tinker, Tailor, Soldier, Spy*] Similarly, when Smiley is forced into retirement at the end of

*WARNING--Plot developments are revealed herein.

15

The Honourable Schoolboy (1977), Guillam is pushed aside again.
Their relationship is one of mutual loyalty never broken, one
against which other relationships in the novels may be measured.
In *The Looking Glass War* (1965), Smiley appears only as a
minor character, as the story focuses on an incompetent and
impoverished rival intelligence agency pathetically attempting
to justify its continued existence by running an agent into
Eastern Europe for the first time since the end of the war.
The head of the agency, Leclerc, is a weak and incompetent
mirror image of Smiley, while his aide, Avery, is a degenerate
version of Guillam. The two of them recruit a Polish immigrant
whom they send into East Germany and abandon, having trained
him inadequately and furnished him with obsolete equipment.
Before this agent leaves England, however, he develops a
"brotherly" affection for Avery and a filial respect for
Leclerc. That these relationships parody the Smiley-Guillam
relationship reinforces the thematic principles of the book:
that the two sides in the cold war are actually mirror images
of each other, and the activities of the intelligence agencies
involved in it are as absurd as battles fought with mirrors.
Le Carré's use of the father-son motif reaches its culmin-
ation in *The Honourable Schoolboy*, in which Jerry Westerby, a
journalist and part-time agent who had been a minor character
in *Tinker, Tailor, Soldier, Spy*, becomes the book's protagonist. Westerby is the son of a British aristocrat who wasted
his fortune in horse racing and high living and died leaving
his family virtually penniless. Westerby adopts Smiley as a
father figure, but substitutes filial loyalty for Smiley's
abstract sense of duty and patriotism: "'You point me, I'll
march,' Jerry had replied. 'Tell me the shots and I'll play
them.'" Gradually, however, Westerby's sympathies shift to
Drake Ko, the Hong Kong tycoon who has become the target of a
Circus kidnap operation. Ko, with his money and his interest
in horse racing, reminds Westerby of his real father; furthermore, Westerby falls in love with Ko's mistress, a woman who
is also under surveillance by the Circus. As his sympathies
shift, Westerby begins to question Smiley's moral values,
realizing that in devoting oneself to an institution like the
Circus, one must also be willing to sacrifice innocent ordinary
people: "Trouble is, sport, the paying is actually done by the
other poor sods." Westerby attempts to prevent Ko's capture
by the Circus and is killed by Smiley's bodyguard. Since the
setting is Southeast Asia during the final days of American
involvement in the Vietnam War, the Smiley-Westerby rupture
suggests the generational schisms which that war created.
Though Smiley's operation in *The Honourable Schoolboy* suc-
ceeds, he once again loses control of the agency--this time
to a faction with CIA backing--and one can't help believing
that his loss of power this time will be permanent. After all,
the death of Westerby, though not his doing, follows naturally
from his loyalty to his beloved Circus. Furthermore, that something like this will eventually happen to Smiley is predictable
from the beginning. In *Call for the Dead* (1961), the first book
in the series, Smiley is forced to kill an East German agent
who had been a key man in one of Smiley's own World War II net-
works and had played the filial role in the father-son relationship that developed between them. Smiley kills him in
hand-to-hand combat, realizing that "Dieter had let him do it,

had not fired the gun, had remembered their friendship when
Smiley had not." Thus, for all his idealism and devotion to
duty, Smiley worships a false god all along, one that from
time to time demands human sacrifice. Westerby rejects this
form of sacrilege and emerges as Smiley's moral superior. We
might conclude, then, that his fall from grace within the Circus carries with it at least a hint of poetic justice.

In *Smiley's People*, Smiley comes out of retirement once
again, this time to conduct a one-man operation which begins
with the investigation of the murder of an ex-agent from
Smiley's past. The investigation culminates in Smiley's en-
gineering the defection of Karla, his opposite number and
former nemesis in the KGB's Moscow Centre. Though the capture
of Karla is Smiley's crowning achievement, he resumes his retirement when the operation is over; he gives no thought to
returning to his former position as head of the Circus. He
even rejects the attempt of a young Circus operative named
Mostyn to hero-worship him: "He did not wish to be this boy's
hero, or to be caressed by his voice, his gaze, his 'sir's."
Mostyn, denied a father-figure, resigns from the service
shortly afterward. As Karla crosses into West Berlin at the
book's end, Smiley is depicted as a weary old man. Guillam,
himself near fifty, proclaims in faintly elegiac terms what
is probably the end of his mentor's career: "Come on, old
friend.... It's bedtime."

Generally, then, the dynastic changes that recur in
Smiley's Circus suggest that modern bureaucratic institutions
are as politically irrational and barbaric as medieval king-
doms. Smiley's exit from the chaos in which he has lived and
reigned is, however, as graceful as that of Tennyson's King
Arthur, who realizes that

> The old order changeth, yielding place to new,
> And God fulfills himself in many ways,
> Lest one good custom should corrupt the world.*

Finally, as an interesting sidelight to le Carré's use of
father-and-son relationships, we might note that le Carré's
own father was imprisoned, an event that cast a shadow over le
Carré's childhood.† We might conjecture that the fictional
fathers and sons are le Carré's attempt to exorcise some of
the devils of his past.

---

*"The Passing of Arthur."
†Le Carré's "Spy Story," *The New York Times Book Review*
(March 12, 1978), 3.

SPY SERIES CHARACTERS IN HARDBACK, VIII

By Barry Van Tilburg

DOSSIER #40: Gregory Sallust.
CREATED BY: Dennis Wheatley.
OCCUPATION: Agent for British intelligence during WWII.
ASSOCIATES: Erika von Osterberg, a Hungarian baroness who lat-
er becomes Sallust's wife; Sir Pellinore Gwaine-Cust, Sal-
lust's boss; Gruppenfuehrer Grauber, Sallust's arch enemy.
WEAPONS: Pistols and rifles.
OTHER COMMENTS: Sallust is a fictional agent dropped into real
history. Chamberlain and Churchill are there. So are
Goering, Goebels, Hess, and Hitler.
The Black Baroness (Hutchinson, 1940).
The Scarlet Imposter (MacMillan, 1942).
Faked Passports (MacMillan, 1943).
V for Vengeance (Hutchinson, 1943).
Come into My Parlour (Hutchinson, 1946).
Traitor's Gate (Hutchinson, 1958).
They Used Dark Forces (Hutchinson, 1964).

DOSSIER #41: Giles Yeoman.
CREATED BY: Martin Woodhouse.
OCCUPATION: Agent for British intelligence department called
Seeker Section.
ASSOCIATES: Major Driver, his boss.
WEAPONS: Anything available.
OTHER COMMENTS: Yeoman is an electronics wizard who gets mixed
up in scientific espionage matters. In the last book, he,
a fellow agent, and Yeoman's girlfriend, all retired, de-
cide to form a company to handle jobs considered impossible.
They charge very high fees so as not to have to work too
often.
Tree Frog (Coward, McCann, 1966).
Bush Baby (Coward, McCann, 1968).
Mama Doll (Coward, McCann, 1972).
Blue Bone (Coward, McCann, 1973).
Moon Hill (Coward, McCann, 1976).

DOSSIER #42: Jonas Wilde.
CREATES BY: Andrew York [Christopher Nicole].
OCCUPATION: Agent for the killing arm of the British secret
service.
ASSOCIATES: Commander Mocka, Wilde's first bos; Sir Gerald
Light, Wilde's second boss; Lady Light, Sir Gerald's wife
and Wilde's mistress.
WEAPONS: Wilde can use guns and knives but prefers his hands.
OTHER COMMENTS: The books are very violent. In the early ones
we find Wilde has killed one of his own people. He used
to just kill whoever he was told to. Now, he needs reasons to kill. He has to know and personally hate his victims. He slowly becomes a broken man, as his friends die
one by one. He turns to drinking. He questions his tal-
ents and himself. In the last books, Wilde couldn't care
less if he survives or not.
The Eliminator (Hutchinson, 1966; Lippincott, 1967).
The Co-Ordinator (Hutchinson, 1967; Lippincott, 1967).

The Predator (Hutchinson, 1967; Lippincott, 1968).
The Deviator (Hutchinson, 1968; Lippincott, 1969).
The Dominator (Hutchinson, 1969).
The Infiltrator (Hutchinson, 1971; Doubleday, 1971).
The Expurgator (Hutchinson, 1972; Doubleday, 1973).
The Captivator (Hutchinson, 1973; Doubleday, 1974).
The Fascinator (Hutchinson, 1975; Doubleday, 1975).

DOSSIER #43: Emily Pollifax.
CREATED BY: Dorothy Gilman (Butters).
OCCUPATION: Part-time agent for the CIA.
ASSOCIATES: Carstairs and Bishop, CIA agents.
WEAPONS: Handbags, hatpins; shoots guns and has even taken up
    karate.
OTHER COMMENTS: A widow in her sixties, Mrs. Pollifax makes a
    very unlikely agent. The CIA figures her age and looks
    are just right for courier woek. She has other ideas,
    which get her into more trouble, but she always manages to
    cope. She has all the little every-day niceties down pat.
    In *The Unexpected Mrs. Pollifax* she even plays solitaire
    while awaiting interrogation by the bad guys. A cool,
    homey type who usually wins in the end.
The Unexpected Mrs. Pollifax (Doubleday, 1966).
The Amazing Mrs. Pollifax (Doubleday, 1970).
The Elusive Mrs. Pollifax (Doubleday, 1971).
A Palm for Mrs. Pollifax (Doubleday, 1973).
Mrs. Pollifax on Safari (Doubleday, 1976).

DOSSIER #44: Max Heald.
CREATED BY: Harry Hossent.
OCCUPATION: Agent for British intelligence.
ASSOCIATES: Johnathan Mortimer, his boss.
WEAPONS: Pistols and rifles.
OTHER COMMENTS: Heald is a very violent killer. In the first
    book he is sent out to find and kill his own wife, who has
    turned traitor. In the last book Heald is kidnapped and
    mentally tortured.
Spies Die at Dawn (John Long, 1958).
No End to Fear (John Long, 1959).
Memory of Treason (John Long, 1961).
Spies Have No Friends (John Long, 1963).
Run for Your Death (John Long, 1965).
The Fear Business (John Long, 1967).

DOSSIER #45: Callan.
CREATED BY: James Mitchell.
OCCUPATION: Counterespionage agent for British intelligence.
ASSOCIATES: Hunter, his boss; Meares, a fellow agent who wants
    Callan's job; Lonely, a friend and helper.
WEAPONS: .38 caliber pistols.
OTHER COMMENTS: In the first book Callan is considered to be
    no longer up to his job and is therefore a risk. He is
    always trying to prove his capabilities and stay alive.
    Hunter puts his file into a red folder, which means that
    he is expendable. In the second book, Callan develops
    medical problems; during his annual physical, he learns
    that his headaches and dizziness are all leading up to
    double vision. Since his eyes are essential to his job,
    his problems become interesting.

Red File for Callan (Simon & Schuster, 1969).
Russian roulette (Morrow, 1973).
Death and Bright Water (Morrow, 1974).
Smear Job (Putnam, 1975).
File on a Willing Victim (The Bell House Book [Hodder], 1975).

DOSSIER #46: Julia Probyn (later Jamieson).
CREATED BY: Ann Bridge.
OCCUPATION: Journalist and amateur agent, she later becomes
    the wife of a British intelligence officer, and through
    her husband and her cousin she keeps getting mixed up in
    intelligence affairs.
ASSOCIATES: Colin Munro, Julia's cousin, an intelligence agent;
    Hugh Torrens, one of Colin's superiors whom she almost
    married; Philip Jamieson, Julia's husband, and another of
    Colin's superiors; Mrs. Hathaway, a very spunky old lady
    friend of Julia's who helps her quite a bit.
WEAPONS: Julia herself uses no weapons other than her brains.
    She leaves the strongarm work to Colin and the police.
OTHER COMMENTS: Julia's inquisitive nature often gets her into
    the thick of things. In the first book she almost gets
    blown up by a bomb meant for Colin. She comes out of it
    with a concussion and a wound which leaves a scar on her
    forehead. In the next to the last book Julia decides it
    is time she went to work for British intelligence and gets
    paid for it; her husband has died on an assignment which
    she herself completes, and now she needs something to oc-
    cupy her mind.
The Lighthearted Quest (MacMillan, 1956; Chatto & Windus, 1956).
The Portuguese Escape (MacMillan, 1958; Chatto & Windus, 1958).
The Numbered Account (McGraw-Hill, 1960; Chatto & Windus, 1960).
The Dangerous Islands (McGraw-Hill, 1963; Chatto & Windus, 1964).
Emergency in the Pyrenees (McGraw-Hill, 1965; Chatto & Windus,
    1965).
The Episode at Toledo (McGraw-Hill, 1966; Chato & Windus,
    1967).
The Malady in Madeira (McGraw-Hill, 1969); Chatto & Windus,
    1970).

DOSSIER #47: Colonel Royston and Peter Castle.
CREATED BY: Gilderoy Davison.
OCCUPATION: Agents for the British secret service, of which
    Royston later becomes Chief.
ASSOCIATES: General Mason, their boss; Bill Castle, Peter's
    brother, who often becomes involved; Ex-Duke Ferdinand,
    "The Man with the Twisted Face," who has many names as
    well; Otto, an ex-cohort of "Twisted Face," they have a
    oneupmanship battle going on in the last three books.
WEAPONS: Revolvers.
OTHER COMMENTS: Royston is an old hand at espionage, having
    been in it since WWI. Castle is a newcomer, recruited by
    Royston at the start of the series. In the first book we
    learn of "The Man with the Twisted Face" and his monstrous
    activities. In the third book we go back in time to learn
    who he is, how his face became disfigured, and the cause
    of his extreme dislike of England and its people.
The Man with the Twisted Face (Herbert Jenkins, 1931).
The Prince of Spies (Herbert Jenkins, 1932).
A Traitor Unmasked (Herbert Jenkins, 1932).

The Devil's Apprentice (Jerbert Jenkins, 1933).
Mystery of the Red-Haired Valet (Herbert Jenkins, 1934).
Twisted Face, the Avenger (Herbert Jenkins, 1935).
Twisted Face Strikes Again (Herbert Jenkins, 1939).
Death in the A.R.P. (Herbert Jenkins, 1939).
Twisted Face Defends His Title (Jenkins, 1940).
A Dogfight with Death (Herbert Jenkins, 1941).
Satan's Satellite (Herbert Jenkins, 1942).

DOSSIER #48: John Meredith.
CREATED BY: Francis Gerard.
OCCUPATION: Meredith starts the series as a chief inspector of
    Scotland Yard, having worked his way up through the ranks.
    In *Secret Sceptre* he retires and is knighted. During
    WWII he works for British Military Intelligence, eventually
    becoming Head of Combined Intelligence.
ASSOCIATES: Sergeant Beef of the CID, his assistant; Inspector
    Bradford, another friend and associate; Juanita, Meredith's
    first wife; McAllistair, Meredith's boss in M.I.; Jill,
    Meredith's second wife.
WEAPONS: Service revolvers.
OTHER COMMENTS: Meredith is a very cool-headed and calm sort
    of person, and he can be hard as nails. He has very un-
    orthodox methods for a policeman, which later help him in
    his intelligence work. His exploits during the war years
    leave him almost a broken man, and upon returning to Eng-
    land he learns of the death of his first wife and his sons
    in an air raid. All he has left is his dog, which he
    clings to to keep hold of the past.
Concrete Castle (Rich & Cowan, 1930).
Number 1-2-3 (Rich & Cowan, 1930).
The Dictatorship of the Dove (Rich & Cowan, 1936).
The Black Emperor (Rich & Cowan, 1936).
Fatal Friday (Rich & Cowan, 1936).
Red Rope (Rich & Cowan, 1937).
Secret Sceptre (Rich & Cowan, 1937).
Prince of Paradise (Rich & Cowan, 1939).
Wotan's Wedge (Rich & Cowan, 1939).
Golden Guilt (Rich & Cowan, 1940).
The Secret of the Sapphire (MacDonald, 1940).
The Mind of John Meredith (MacDonald, 1946).
Sorcerer's Shaft (MacDonald, 1947).
Prisoner of the Pyramid (MacDonald, 1948).
Flight into Fear (MacDonald, 1948).
Transparent Traitor (MacDonald, 1949).
The Promise of the Phoenix (MacDonald, 1950).
Bare Bodkin (MacDonald, 1951).

It's About Crime

By Marvin Lachman

PRESIDENT NERO WOLFE

It is only fitting that Rex Stout, who caused so much con-
sternation in Sherlockian circles with his monograph "Watson
Was a Woman," should have similar scrutiny paid to his work.
There has been a small, but increasing, amount of scholarship
devoted to Stout and his famous creation. Bernard De Voto's
"Alias Nero Wolfe," which appeared in the July 1954 issue of
Harper's, was a brief biography. Dr. John D. Clark's "Some
Notes Relating to a Preliminary Investigation into the Pater-
nity of Nero Wolfe" in *The Baker Street Journal* for January
1956 focused on one aspect of Wolfe's life, that which would
most appeal to Sherlockians. William Baring-Gould's *Nero
Wolfe of West Thirty-fifth Street* (1969) was a book-length
discussion of Wolfe, similar to one the author had done regarding Holmes. Baring-Gould also stresses the connection
between Holmes and Wolfe.

More recently, John McAleer's *Rex Stout* (1978) is the de-
finitive biography of Wolfe's creator, with many references
to the creation. Guy Townsend's "Nero Wolfe Saga" in TMF
chronicled every case on which Wolfe worked.

Surprisingly, none of these perceptive scholars showed
they were aware of the fact that Rex Stout, for four decades,
thought of Nero Wolfe as President of the United States.

Stout's interest in the U.S. Presidency predated Wolfe.
As a young enlisted man in the Navy he served as a yeoman
aboard Theodore Roosevelt's yacht. In 1908 he sold the New
York *World* a piece analyzing the palm prints of Presidential
nominee William Howard Taft. Just prior to starting the Nero
Wolfe series, Stout published *The President Vanishes* (1934).
Set in the near future, during a time of domestic turmoil, it
tells of the kidnapping of a President who has opposed a cabal
of industrialists and politicians who have been fomenting a
revolution.

It is clear that in his own mind Stout identified Nero
Wolfe with the current President of the United States. Time
after time he gives Wolfe situations and dialogue which are
irrelevant to the work of a detective, but not to the func-
tioning of the President. In the very first Wolfe novel,
Fer-de-Lance, we have Nero and Archie discussing financial
crises, borrowing, and the Gold Reserve. This discussion is
very similar to real conferences, reported by Schlesinger in

The Coming of the New Deal, between Franklin Roosevelt and his Treasury Secretary, William H. Woodin, regarding these subjects.

We learn in *The Rubber Band* that Stout really regarded Wolfe's residency as the White House. Archie says after Wolfe has entertained the Marquis of Clivers, whom they consider a possible murderer, "I suspect that noblemen and people who eat lunch at the White House commit more than their share of murders compared to their numerical strength in the total population." In the novelet "Cop Killer" Archie notices two tourists staring at Wolfe's house as if it were the White House. In another novelet, "Cordially Invited to Meet Death," Archie bursts in on Wolfe in conference. He says, "They looked around at me as I would expect to be looked at if I busted into a cabinet meeting at the White House."

One wonders if his feeling as to what Wolfe's real residence should be was behind Stout's surprisingly clumsy attempts to hide the exact locale. After all, he gave nine different numbers for the house on West Thirty-fifth Street. The telephone was Pennsylvania 3-1212, a clear clue since the White House is, of course, on Pennsylvania Avenue. Another clue is in "The Fourth of July Picnic," Wolfe's only reference to the purchase of his home. This is Stout's symbolic reference to the fact that, due to events which began on a July Fourth, American Presidents have come to reside in the White House.

Though continuing to tell detective stories in which Wolfe serves individual clients, Stout was coming to regard the people of the United States as Wolfe's true clients. In 1937, FDR was making slow inroads in the area of civil rights, saying in a speech at the time: "People like you and me are fighting and must continue to fight for the day when a man will be regarded as a man regardless of his race or faith or country.... That day will come, but we must pass through perilous times before we realize it." FDR's speech expressed sentiments similar to those spoken by Wolfe to the Negro waiters in *Too Many Cooks*, set in April 1937: "The ideal human agreement is one in which distinctions of race and color and religion are totally disregarded; anyone helping to preserve those discinctions is postponing that ideal...."

Though U.S. foreign policy was officially neutral regarding the Spanish civil war, it was clear that FDR favored the Loyalists over the Fascists. In *Over My Dead Body*, set in November 1938, Wolfe expresses similar sentiments and even makes a financial contribution to the Loyalists.

During *Where There's a Will*, set in the summer of 1939, a client says to Wolfe, "You sould like a Bolshevik," echoing a charge that many right-wingers made about Roosevelt. In the same book Archie says, "Nero Wolfe had gone in for a series of fantastic expenditures ... a personal and intimate test of the operations of the New Deal WPA." Strange talk regarding a man whose job ostensibly is to solve mysteries.

In the novelets writted by Stout during World War II, we are given descriptions of Wolfe studying maps. These descriptions are remarkably similar, according to Barbara Tuchman and others, to those of FDR studying war-time maps. Archie is referred to by Wolfe as his "Secretary of War." In "Not Quite Dead Enough" Stout describes a meeting between Wolfe and a statesman who sounds like Churchill!

When Harry S Truman became President in 1945, Stout undoubtedly had difficulty in identifying Wolfe with that President. Both FDR and Wolfe had lacked mobility. The former due to polio; the latter by choice. Truman, on the other hand, was an active Mid-westerner, a man who loved to walk. A perfect description of Archie, and Stout began to see Goodwin as the President. Stout had already been thinking of Archie in those terms. In "Booby Trap," set in August 1943, he has Archie say, "I could never run for President." One of the most personal parallels concerns the habit Truman and Goodwin shared of washing out their own socks. Merle Miller quoted Truman as saying, "one of the things everybody had to do for himself was to wash his own socks." He did this even after becoming President. So, in Stout's mind, did Archie.

If Stout were trying to keep his views about Wolfe/Goodwin and the Presidency secret, he did a poor job. An incredible lapse occurs during *Too Many Women*, set in March 1947. A none-too-bright clerical employee actually says to Archie: "Mr. Truman, do you know of any jobs where you don't have to spell?"

The Second Confession takes place shortly after Truman's successful 1948 campaign. It is decidedly anti-Henry A. Wallace, referring to Communist takeover of Wallace's Progressive Party. That third party was one of the factors which had made Truman so great an underdog against Dewey. In the same book, Archie refers to Stalin as "Uncle Joe," the same joking reference to the dictator that Truman used. Wolfe puts pressure on Harvey, a tall, thin Communist with a mustache, to disclose someone's Party membership in order to solve a murder.

In the 1951 novelet "Home to Roost," Wolfe does something similar, lecturing Heath, a trustee of the Communist Party's bail fund who won't disclose names needed in a murder investigation. There is a great similarity in both cases, beyond physical description and first initial, to the case of Dashiell Hammett, who was imprisoned for contempt in refusing to disclose names of Communists. Was Stout lecturing a thinly-disguised fellow mystery writer in his stories? "Home to Roost" also sees Wolfe emulating Truman's position of being simultaneously anti-Communist and yet against the McCarthy-type witch hunt. He deplores the tendency to accuse people of pro-Communism irresponsibly (such charges had been levelled against Truman's Secretary of State, Dean Acheson).

In the 1950 novelet "Door to Death" we have Archie say, prophetically, "not being a candidate for President," first intimation of Truman's ultimate decision not to seek reelection in 1952. *Prisoner's Base* takes place in June 1952, while the Republican National Convention is going on. We find Wolfe and Archie analyzing the candidates for the Republican nomination. The outgoing, but loyally Democratic, President considering his party's potential opposition.

Watchers of male fashions will recall that in January 1953 Eisenhower broke a tradition by wearing a homburg, instead of the usual top hat, to his inauguration. In *The Golden Spiders,* set in 1953, we view Archie, for the first and only time, wearing a homburg.

By this time Stout was using Wolfe and Archie interchangeably regarding his Presidential parallels. In *The Black Mountain,* set in March-April 1954, Wolfe, like Eisenhower, decides not to support "freedom" movements in Yugoslavia against Tito, recognizing that if Tito were overthrown, Russia would take

over the country. He opines that "Saul Panzer could flummox
Tito and Malenkov put together." In the same book, reacting
to the men who bedeviled Eisenhower abroad and at home, Wolfe
openly criticizes both Georgi Malenkov, then leader of the
USSR, and Senator Joe McCarthy.

In November 1956 the Suez crisis and war in the Middle
East were major concerns to President Eisenhower. During that
month, in *Might as Well Be Dead*, Wolfe and Archie conduct two
conversations on these matters which bear no relation to the
plot of the mystery.

In 1958's "The Fourth of July Murder," Stout has Wolfe
leave his home to address the Independence Day picnic of a
labor union. That is the action of a politically aware President, but not of an agoraphobic. On a more trivial level,
Plot It Yourself in May 1959 has the only instance of Archie
watching a cowboy show on TV. Eisenhower was known as a great
fan of Westerns.

In the Spring of 1960 a summit conference was called off
because of the famous U-2 incident. Eisenhower admitted to
our having spied over the USSR. *Too Many Clients*, set at that
time, has Archie saying: "I would like to be present to see
his [Fred Durkin's] face if and when Wolfe tells him to go to
Moscow and tail Kruschev." Earlier, regarding a meeting that
did take place, Archie had said, in *Champagne for One*, "while
I reported on the summit conference ...."

The Final Deduction, in 1961, opens with Wolfe glaring at
his big globe, especially Cuba and Laos, two trouble spots
which concerned President Kennedy. Recently, many revelations
have been made regarding the sex life of Kennedy. Was Stout
privy to secret information when, in *The Mother Hunt*, he
actually has a scene in which Wolfe is alone in a bedroom with
a woman?

Early in the Lyndon Johnson administration (*A Right to Die*
in February 1964) we see Archie discussing Rockefeller and
Goldwater, the two men who would vie for the Republican nomination to run against LBJ. Wolfe discusses Viet Nam at dinner
in *Death of a Doxy* in January 1966. Since Johnson of Texas
was our most notable "Western" President, it is not as amazing
as it otherwise would be to see Nero Wolfe (as we do in *Death
of a Dude* in August 1968) "roughing it" in Wyoming.

In *Please Pass the Guilt*, set in the summer of 1969, we
read, "The Vice-President and his secretary came on the dot at
half past two. Precisely." We also have a wealthy woman attempting, unsuccessfully, to speak to Wolfe. "My god," she
said, "you might think he's the President." Stout thinks he
is, as he did earlier in the novelet "Immune to Murder."
There, Stout has Wolfe say, "I must first speak to the Secretary of State on the telephone. If he is not in Washington,
he must be located." Only the President, not even Nero Wolfe,
would speak in so peremptory a manner. It is in *Please Pass
the Guilt* that we have Wolfe growl after putting down *The
Palace Guard* by Dan Rather and Gary Gates, a book critical of
the Nixon Presidency.

The last Wolfe novel, *A Family Affair*, is set in 1974,
just before Nixon resigned. Archie, in language uncharacter-
istic of him (but typical of the Nixon inner circle), says,
"I didn't have the slightest idea of his game plan.... I want
to make it perfectly clear." Later, Archie says about Wolfe:
"He probably knew more about every angle of Watergate than any

dozen of his fellow citizens, for instance the first names of
Haldeman's grandparents.

During this book we get an analogy between five indicted
Nixon aides and the Stout team of five (Wolfe, Archie, Panzer,
Durkin, and Orrie Cather). We have Wolfe devising a strategy
for his team that can only be regarded as "stonewalling." We
even have a lawyer, described as sounding and looking like
John Mitchell, say to Wolfe: "I'm surprised that you don't
seem to realize what you're trying to do. You're trying to
get us to go along with you on a cover-up."

Stout was quoted as being critical of Nixon and Watergate,
yet in a 1974 story in the *Washington Post* by Lawrence Meyer,
Wolfe talks to Nixon about the famous 18½ minutes of tape.
The Watergate-related *Family Affair* shows Stout finally had
Nero Wolfe identify too strongly with the wrong president.
Nero Wolfe never took on another case. He was to be the final
victim of Watergate.

Mystery * File

Short Reviews
By Steve Lewis

Loren D. Estleman. *Motor City Blues*. Houghton Mifflin, 1980, 219 pp., $9.95.

Say welcome to a new private eye. Amos Walker hails from Detroit., and if nothing else, it insures he has no shortage of clients.

He's hired by an ex-gangster named Ben Morningstar to find his missing ward. The only clue is a black-and-white glossy of the type sold under the counter in even "those" kinds of bookstores.

He's also a witness to the kidnapping of an old "friend," a former company commander back in the days of the Vietnam affair. In broad daylight, on Woodward Avenue. I believe it.

There's more. The Black Legion--a northern offshoot of the Klan--may be involved in the death of a militant young black labor leader. It's quite a case.

Nothing wholly original, mind you, and if coincidence bothers you, stay away. All the same, it's written with a definite sense of style and a contagious feeling for the rhythms of life in the inner city.

If you're from out of town, you might even get the feeling that the grand old city of Detroit is nothing but one gigantic slum, ready and ripe for redevelopment. Well, I've been there, and do you know--not meaning to malign one of my favorite cities at all--I can tell you this: you'd not really be so very far from wrong. (B)

Randy Striker. *Key West Connection*. Signet, 1981, 164 pp., $1.95.

Here's the first installment of a brand new "action-packed" adventure series. The hero is Floridian charterboat captain Dusky MacMorgan, ex-U.S. Navy (underwater demolition). He's a cross between Travis McGee and Don Pendleton's Mack Bolan, if you can believe it. He leaves a lot of dead people behind him.

And, of course, so do the villains. In this book they're a gang of dope smugglers. The top levels of the gang include a U.S. Senator (unnamed) and assorted top officials in all levels of the executive branch. And an ounce of humanity you would not find in any of them.

MacMorgan's wife and twin little boys are killed in a bomb
accident (it was meant for him), and he takes his remorse out
in total retaliation. He leaves a lot of dead people behind.
(Or did I say that?)

I think Randy Striker (is that really his name?) should
quit the annoying habit of telling the end of the chapter
first. Otherwise, well, you probably already know if you're
going to go out looking for this or not. If Striker is also
the charterboat captain we are told he is, these are--if
you'll excuse the expression--his wet dreams. (C minus)

Wilson Tucker. *To Keep or Kill*. Rinehart, 1947, 186 pp.

Tucker, who is probably better known today for his science
fiction, wrote a total of five Charles Horne mysteries for
Rinehart back between 1946 and 1951. After that he apparently
decided he was better off not trying to write detective fiction, even as a sideline.

Not that he left the field completely, but I think he probably made the right decision.

Horne is a private eye. Most of his work is done for in-
surance companies. He quite vehemently does not do divorce
work. The small metropolis of Boone, Illinois, where he has
his office, is a figment of Tucker's imagination, although
there *is* a Boone County (up near Rockford).

This is the second Horne book. As it begins, he is witness to an explosion. He thinks it's a practical joke at
first, but when it goes off it takes part of a city block and
a couple of victims with it. Later, Horne is kidnapped and
kept a prisoner in the home of the girl who planted the bomb.
She's a redhead, tall, beautiful, and as loopy as a loon.

She is in love with Horne, she has been stalking him for
months, and now that she "owns" him, so to speak, she expects
... well, this was written before such explicit intentions
could be stated, but those are the kinds of intentions she
has. Viewed from today's more permissive perspective, Horne's
brave resistance to temptation seems both admirable and re-
freshingly naive.

Tucker's style in this book is a burbling, slap-happy one,
somewhat reminiscent of Fredric Brown in nature. In all, however, it hardly manages to disguise a total apparent lack of
respect for logical thought processes. Or let me put it another way: the sort of logic that is used by all concerned
would make sense only to the well-confined inmates of a luna-
tic asylum.

It wouldn't be hard to enjoy this quirky excuse for a detective story immensely. There is a thin line, it is said,
between genius and lunacy. If I'd been able to follow the
plot at all, I'd have said this was the work of the former.
As for a letter grade, I'm not too sure of this one at all,
but if it means anything to you, what I'm going to do, if I
don't change my mind tomorrow, is give this book a definite--
(C plus?)

Mary Fitt. *Mizmaze*. Penguin, 1961, 175 pp.

Some people have been recommending Mary Fitt to me as an

author to try. This is fine with me. I'm always looking for
someone new who's worth reading. But. This is the one that
was handy, this is the one I tried, and I'm sorry, I can't
help it--it's awful. Now they tell me it's her worst book.
No kidding. I can believe it. I can't ever recall reading
anything as bad as this. (Of course, with a tip of the hat to
Bill Pronzini, I've never yet quite managed to read a Phoenix
Press mystery, either.

Fitt's police detective is Superintendent Mallett. In
this case he investigates the death of a man in a maze. Cause
of death, the old standby, the blunt instrument. More specifically, a mallet. (The superintendent acknowledges, but does
not appreciate, the obvious play on words.)

Not a bad beginning, by any means, but here's where any
similarity to a rigorous police procedural ends. Mallett
stays to guard the body until his men arrive, and in the mean-
time his friend Dr. Fitzbrown is the one who casually questions all the suspects. And there's a house full of them.
Mallett, however, is content to be filled in later. By page
84, with this total lack of official attention so strangely
thrust upon them, the friends and family of the dead man take
it upon themselves to start traipsing off all over the country-
side.

As Mallett and Fitzbrown seem to have it, the murderer
followed the dead man into the maze; or, it's not quite clear,
was it that he was lying in wait for him instead? Maybe I'm
dense, but it depends, apparently, on which page you happen to
be reading. (See pages 18 and 24 of this Penguin edition, for
example.)

I didn't finish the book. I quit early, soon after, as a
matter of fact, the good doctor's long, passionate, kissing
scene with one of the leading suspects, the dead man's loudly
non-devoted, non-loving daughter. (Side comment: would I allow a hard-boiled private eye to get away with this? Maybe I
would. In the context of what is meant, I assume, to be form-
al investigative proceedings, it's so bizarrely out of character, it's absolutely ridiculous.)

Perhaps I'm measuring this book against the wrong set of
standards, but it just doesn't jell. Malarkey is still malarkey, no matter what kind of jar it comes in. (F)

Jack S. Scott. *The Gospel Lamb.* Harper & Row, 1980, 167 pp.,
$9.95.

The career of Detective Sergeant Rosher has certainly had
its ups and downs. He was last heard from in *A Clutch of Vip-
ers*, in which a "family" he takes into his household turns out
to be a gang of fornicators and thieves set upon him by a top
echelon hoodlum with a vicious sense of humor. He now needs
to put in only two more years before he can retire with full
pension, and only by special dispensation is he allowed to do
so.

And with a pop festival nearly surrounding the village of
Burton Danvers, and every man available urgently needed, he
welcomes the chance to get his suffering bottom out and away
from the endless shuffle of paperwork.

Not to mention the opportunity of viewing the breathtaking
sight of all those bare, bobbing breasts. The music is not

nearly the attraction as is provided by the combined lure of bright sun, rampant drugs, and free sex. What worries the constabulary most, however, is how this veritable nest of iniquity is also bound to attract the attention of the area's notorious prostitute killer, the self-styled Avenger.

A kaleidoscope of crimes follows: many minor, one major. The only question is whether the dead girl is the Avenger's latest victim, or merely the responsibility of some other poor dolt strung out on LSD.

There is one surprise twist that still awaits, at least, but otherwise from here on out the story largely plays itself out on its own. I liked the carefree atmosphere of the first half, myself, much more than the sour-tasting nastiness that follows. Still, very nearly in spite of himself, Rosher manages to nab some of the glory himself this time.

What I did miss was the touch of sympathetic understanding that up to now has always belied Scott's otherwise unflaggingly cynical attitude toward the world. Recommended, therefore, only to those who've been following the series, and want to see what sort of pitfall Rosher steps into next, or those wholly tolerant of the aftertaste of ashes. (C)

Charles L. Clifford. *While the Bells Rang.* Doubleday/Crime Club, 1941, 275 pp.

Except for one borderline item, according to *Hubin* this book constitutes the extent of Clifford's contribution to novel-length crime fiction. (According to the dust jacket, he was well known for his short stories, but if any of them were detective stories, I'm embarrassed to say I don't know.)

When the story begins, a great deal has already happened. A well-known columnist has been murdered on a polo-player's ranch, and an army captain from the base adjoining has already been tried and convicted. Convinced of his innocence, however, his fiancee and his closest army buddy decide to become partners and do a little bit of undercover detective work to prove it.

The delivery is fast and slangy--the combined effect, I imagine, of the army post background plus the presence of the fast-paced horsey set next door--while at times a little too much is left unsaid, making the whole affair seem to be taking place in another time and another place altogether. Through the faulty focus of this self-contained time-machine, it's no great wonder the pieces of the puzzle seem continually blurred and fractionally out of place.

And yet, before it was all over, the characters had started to show definite signs of life, and some of their romantic entanglements had begun to seem important to me as well as to them.

If Clifford had been able to give his amateur sleuths a little more direction, if he had gathered his own material a little more tightly together, if he'd forced the plot to ramble a little less, I'm convinced he'd have had a winner.

That's a lot of "ifs," I grant you. I was left in a good mood when it was over, though, and I really think he came closer than I thought for a while he was going to. (B minus)

Dashiell Hammett. *The Maltese Falcon*. From *The Novels of Dashiell Hammett*. Knopf, 1965. Originally published in 1930.

    I don't suppose I have to convince you to read this book, do I? If you haven't read it yet, I don't suppose you will. Maybe I'm wrong. Maybe you've never gotten around to it. It would be easy to do. But remember, nobody lives forever. You've only got one life to live, and that's all you've got. (A)
COMMENTS:
    1. The part of Sam Spade was made for Humphrey Bogart.
    2. John Huston was wise to write the part of Rhea Gutman out of the screenplay.
    3. Spade's mind always seems to be several jumps ahead of the story, but Barzun and Taylor call him "repeatedly stupid." Why?
    4. Likeable, I'm not so sure he is.

Richard Hugo. *Death and the Good Life*. St. Martin's, 1981, 215 pp., $10.95.

    Hugo is a noted American poet, and this is his first mystery. His hero is a soft-hearted ex-cop from Seattle, and his name is Al Barnes. Since quitting his job in the city, he's taken a deputy sheriff's position in the small town of Plains, Montana.
    That's right. Montana. Not Georgia. The Pacific Northwest is rapidly becoming a hotbed of detective-story activity. You can add another pretty good one to the list.
    The first murder is an axe-killing, and so's the second, but it doesn't seem to fit the pattern. The trail leads Barnes back to Oregon, and once there, deep into the past. It takes a gut feeling for the truth to work a scent almost twenty years old, and that Barnes has. Memories are not always pleasant ones, but some of the ones he dredges up are particularly nasty ones.
    The prose is right, and Barnes's instincts for the job are never far from wrong, but the story still doesn't click the way it's supposed to. Strangely enough, it's the rhythm, the beat, that's off. This is essentially a private eye story, and it's a crucial factor. This one just misses. (B minus)* (*Reviews so marked have appeared earlier in the Hartford *Courant*.)

Timothy Harris. *Good Night and Good-bye*. Dell, 1979, 289 pp. $2.25.

    A book more solidly "in the Raymond Chandler tradition" is hard to imagine. From the opening impact of the first page of Chapter One to the ending that comes as inevitably as the passage of time to its sadly depressing conclusion, there is no doubt at all that Timothy Harris has read, devoured, and assimilated the complete works of the master.
    This is not meant as disparagement. The tone and style are Chandler's. The prose and dialogue are not, quite, but if they aren't, they are Harris's own, in a revised and updated

typically Californian tale of modern morality.

Private eye Thomas Kyd, like his Elizabethan namesake, may
have a talent for melodrama, but he lives it as well, instead
of just telling it. There is a girl named Laura, and it is
she whom the story is about. She is a junkie, and a liar, and
she is in trouble. She meets Kyd, who helps, but she marries
a wealthy movie writer named Paul Sassari instead. He is murdered soon after. As she says, "People don't get much out of
knowing me."

Kyd is a master of lost causes, a Sir Galahad on horse-
back, a champion of ladies in distress, but, as he soon dis-
covers, he is not truly a denizen of the fast, jet-paced
world of drugs, easy money, and expensive women. On the other
hand, since he *is* familiar with life in the shade of shabby
sidewalks and sordid secrets, he almost makes out okay.

Finer entertainment for the confirmed private eye afic-
ionado is also hard to imagine. (A)

Janice Law. *Death Under Par*. Houghton Mifflin, 1981, 234 pp.,
    $9.95.

With the obvious exception of horse-racing, I think more
mysteries have had to do with golf than with any other sport.
(And horse-racing is so crooked that there's no way I'd personally ever consider it a sport.)

But golf is the obvious runner-up, and that is what leads
us to the latest Anna Peters thriller. She and long-time boy
friend Harry have finally tied the know, and for their honeymoon they travel to Scotland, for a working vacation during
the British Open--he's an artist on assignment for *Sports Illustrated*.

There have been vandals at work, however, and threats have
been made against one of the golfers. In case you haven't
been following Miss Peters' adventures, she runs her own
security business, and it quickly becomes a working honeymoon
for her as well.

She finds a common thread between the golfer and two of
her leading suspects: they all attended the same small college
in Hartford (Trinity College, recognizably incognito).

As a result, there is a good deal of local Connecticut
scenery involved as well, including a quickie tour through the
offices of the same newspaper that prints most of my reviews.
Which, of course, interested me much more than it will
most of you. A straightforward crime story, which is what
this is, is more realistic than the puzzle artifices of a pure
whodunit, perhaps, but in all truth this case of Anna Peters
presents no other challenge than that of sheer endurance.

A twist was needed. This one comes straight. (C)

Emma Lathen. *Going for the Gold*. Simon and Schuster, 1981,
    251 pp., $11.95.

Reading this latest adventure of banker-detective John
Putnam Thatcher is something like finding yourself caught up
in a huge science-fictional time warp. The Winter Olympics
have always had more visual appeal than Wall Street will ever
have, but to enhance it even further, Miss Lathen relates the

story of a snowbound Lake Placid as it might have happened, in some alternate universe adjoining ours only tangentially.

Imagine, if you will, any or all of the following: the presence of a mad sniper who picks off a French ski-jumper in mid-air; a popular female skier who is falsely accused of taking drugs; a scandal in procurement kickbacks; and the kidnapping of the acting president of the IOC by an entourage of angry Swiss athletes. In their anxiety to cover the inspired performance of the U.S. hockey team, ABC-TV and all of the other media seem to have missed everything else that was going on!

Sloan Guaranty Trust's greatest concern, however, is an incoming flood of counterfeit Eurochecks. Since the intricacies of the forging operation are also essential to uncovering the killer's identity, it's a case right down Thatcher's alley, if no one else's. This one small quibble aside, the rest of the proceedings are happily infused with equal doses of impalusibility and *deja vu*, and then laced with a good healthy belt of wry--humor, that is. (B minus*)

Erle Stanley Gardner. *The Case of the Lazy Lover*. Ballantine, 1981, 218 pp., 1981. First published in 1947.

Ballantine has somehow recently obtained the rights to the enormous output of ESG mystery fiction, including, if my computations are correct, those he wrote as A.A. Fair as well. (Publicity releases mention 120 novels, and I don't think there are nearly that many Perry Mason stories--though to some of you it may seem like it.)

Perry Mason it was, however, who introduced me to "adult" mystery fiction--assuming you can exclude the inevitable batch of Sherlock Holmes stories that everybody read as a kid, didn't they?--and I've had a weakness for his cases ever since. It's been a while since I actually read one, though, so I read this one with a little bit of a question mark niggling in my mind. Have my tastes changed? Is Gardner's functional writing style now slipped beneath me?

Nope. Not really. I notice it, his writing style, more now, and I can see more clearly what he's doing when he does it, but I can assure you that the formula still works. I enjoyed this book, and I'm going to read more of them.

Start with a mystery, grab the reader's attention right away, and don't let go until you're done. That was Gardner's motto, and here's a fine example of the kind of results you can get from that sort of story-telling philosophy. Mason gets two checks for $2500 from the same person, previously unknown, on the same day. One proves to be a forgery.

Add a possible amnesia victim. Various corporate power struggles and legal shenanigans follow galore. Plus a murder, complete with detailed map. Once again circumstantial evidence is shown to be worth about the same as any other pack of lies. And the beginning chapter's events are not explained until the very end.

Except for minor details and occasional changes in the law and police procedures between then and now, the Mason stories are very nearly timeless, and I'm glad to see them back in print again. I can understand if you don't personally care for them. If I may speak on behalf of the rest of us, however, you have our most sincere sympathies! (B)

Verdicts
(More Reviews)

Emma Lathen. *Going for the Gold.* Simon and Schuster, 1981.

It must be a mixed blessing, actually, for an author (or in this case, authors; "Emma Lathen" is really Martha Henissart and Mary Jane Latsis) to acquire a large following of admiring fans. On the one hand, there's an eager audience, ready and waiting for each new book. On the other hand, that same audience has developed certain expectations for each new volume, and it must be hard to top one success with another and yet another. In the case of the Lathen team, they have usually met this goal, satisfying the expectations of their audience for intelligent plotting, intricate (but clearly explained) financial maneuvering, sharp social satire, and keen wit. *Going for the Gold* meets the first two requirements but doesn't quite fulfill the latter pair of expectations.

As official bank to the Winter Olympics, the Sloan has opened temporary branches in the Lake Placid vicinity, and ebullient Bradford Withers, president of the Sloan Guaranty Trust, is serving as a member of the International Olympic Committee. Knowing the smoothness of the Sloan's operation (thanks to its senior officer and Lathen's protagonist, John Putnam Thatcher) and the bumbling nature of Brad Withers' activities, seasoned readers would expect impeccable banking and fumbling Olympic events. Surprisingly, however, both the Sloan and the Games run into foul weather--figuratively and literally. The Sloan gets stung with faked European travellers' checks and a contestant gets shot to death in the midst of a brilliant performance in the ski jump. Thatcher, naturally, sets out to solve both problems. Doing so is complicated by a fairly generous cast of Olympic contestants of several nationalities and varying degrees of brilliance, Lathen's usual clever and useful local cop, and a raft of folk from the Sloan. An immobilizing blizzard twists the plot of the novel and the plot of the criminal simultaneously. All this complexity is fairly satisfying as is the final unraveling of the mysteries, for luckily, the climax is the best part of the book: brisk, tense, full of suspense.

This time out, however, the characters are less clearly defined, the action in the early chapters a bit slow, and the social satire mainly missing--perhaps because the authors do not know their territory so well as usual. A few pot shots at teenagers and at the Olympic Committee aren't enough to meet the Lathen team's usual standards.

What I really missed, however, were the howlingly funny
scenes so central to many of the earlier books; here, a few
brief smiles were the best I could muster until late in the
novel when Everett Gabler (one of the series' funniest, best-
crafted characters) runs afoul of a well-meaning lady who
doesn't grasp his name correctly, and, with his usual attention to detail, insists on keeping Thatcher attached to an un-
attractive, touristy pair of salt and pepper shakers which the
senior officer has purchased only to expedite questioning a
witness. Still, as with the action, the humor mounts with the
suspense of the climax, and the books ends better than it
began.

Not vintage Lathen, *Going for the Gold* is still well worth
reading, but it shouldn't win first prize . . . more like a
bronze! (Jane S. Bakerman)

Margaret Yorke. *The Scent of Fear*. St. Martin's, 1980.

There is plenty of suspense, a lot of action, and some
marvelous characterization in Margaret Yorke's new inverted
mystery, *The Scent of Fear*. More and more, her studies in
tension and psychology are proving to be even more engrossing
than her straight detective stories. In this novel, she provides a whole gallery of fine portraits, ranging from a vic-
iously selfish teenaged pyromaniac through his gentle but determined aunt, her sedate lover, and a well-meaning but ex-
hausting do-gooder, to an aged widow living in a big old house
well isolated from the English village of Framingham, setting
of the story.

Mrs. Anderson, the elderly woman who is the protagonist of
the main plot, is determined to maintain her independence and
her home against the pressures of time and growing infirmity,
even though her efforts are complicated by the increasing difficulty of village life--various services are disappearing,
and she is thrown into more and more reliance upon her own
physical resources at the very time in her life when they are
diminishing. Her antagonists are two. The chief of them is
Kevin Timms, layabout and freeloader, whose bursts of savage
temper result, from time to time, in devastating fires and
even murder. Mrs. Anderson't second antagonist is the well-
intentioned Mureal Dean, who becomes interested in the old
lady and plans to help her, be the help wanted or not. When
Kevin establishes an outpost in the unused upper floors of the
Victorian mansion and Muriel establishes a beachhead in the
sitting room, problems are bound to follow. Muriel's forays
are only all too well known to Mrs. Anderson, while Kevin's
are secret--until the old woman and the violent lad are
marooned together in the house during a blizzard; at that
point, the threat of death becomes all too clear and the tension is terrific.

As is often the case in a Yorke suspense novel, several
love stories are contrasted. Kevin's coarse and casual courtship of Marilyn Green is contrasted with the quiet but certain
courtship of his aunt, Jessie Swales, by Bob Watson, a widower.
Jessie and Bob also provide contrast for another couple, Howard
Dean, Muriel's husband, and Janet Finch, a young widow with a
small daughter. Bob puts his adultery down to Muriel's pre-

occupation with various local activities, but even this trite excuse is individualized by Yorke's skill at characterization. Bob, Muriel, and Janet are real people, likable and disagreeable in turns, and Yorke makes us understand and feel for them all. She does as much for Jessie, whose happiness is threatened by Kevin's anger and resentment, and for Bob, who is far from perfect but who is also deeply understanding and loyal. Marilyn is a pitiable kid neither clever nor pretty and is exploited by almost every person who touches her life.

Taken all in all, these relationships are skillfully balanced; characterizations are well-maintained, and the action is dispensed neatly and deftly at all the right times. *The Scent of Fear* may just be Margaret Yorke's best novel to date. (Jane S. Bakerman)

Joe Lansdale. *Act of Love*. Zebra Books, 1981, 301 pp., $2.75.

I had better say right from the beginning that *Act of Love* is not a book for those who like their murders tidy and antiseptic, nor is it for those who prefer to read about little old ladies who solve crimes over a cup of tea. It is, in fact, one of the most graphic books on "ripper-type" killings that I have ever read; and that's what gives it its power. The "Houston Hacker" is a madman, and his acts are those of a madman. Joe Lansdale doesn't flinch from depicting the man or his acts. The plot is simple--will the police, led by black cop Marvin Hanson, catch the Hacker? And who is the Hacker? I won't spoil things by answering those two questions. I'll just say that the suspense in the book is terrific. You'll read the last third of it in record time, and you might even find that you're holding your breath. It would make a great movie. (Bill Crider)

Samuel Edwards. *The Vidocq Dossier*. Houghton Mifflin, 1977.

As Edwards explains, it is difficult to write a biography of Francois Eugene Vidocq, for the man's life history is a mixture of truth and colorful myth. Vidocq himself promoted many of the outrageous stories, romanticizing his exploits and striking fear into the hearts of lawbreakers. But following Edwards along the obscure trail, we learn many fascinating facts about the world's first detective.

Vidocq was born in 1775 in Arras, France. He was an intelligent child, by nine learning Greek, Latin, and the principles of chemistry and physics. At twelve years he was a master with the sword and pistol. Unfortunately, a keen sense of adventure combined with a weakness for a pretty face led him in and out of trouble countless times. While serving a short jail sentence for a minor infraction at the age of twenty, he committed another crime, forging the pardon of a cell mate. Rather than face more time in prison for the second offense, Vidocq made his escape.

Several times he attempted an honest living, only to be recognized and imprisoned again. With each escape and recapture the sentence was extended and the confinements grew worse, to the point where, on the original charge of forgery, he was shackled with hardened criminals. During his years as a

fugative, Vidocq learned every trick of the trade and made
many acquaintances. His miraculous escapes earned him the
respect and awe of the underworld. When a farsighted police
official offered him the chance to become a free man, Vidocq
turned informer.

Before Vidocq, the police force contained no trained in-
vestigators, and criminals made a mockery of the system.
Vidocq utilized methods of disguise and took advantage of
criminal contacts, techniques previously unheard of. His pe-
culiar expertise soon gave him the most effective arrest and
conviction rate. Even so, it took years of dangerous undercover work to persuade the French Ministry that a plainclothes
detective bureau, separate from the uniformed police, was
needed. In October, 1812, the Brigade de la Surete was established, later serving as a prototype for Scotland Yard and
other investigative departments. Among the many innovations
Vidocq pioneered were handwriting analysis, fingerprinting,
and maintaining files of a criminal's past record. He dabbled
with blood tests, ballistics, and was responsible for the
first known autopsy, clearing an innocent man in the process.
Stool pigeons were the mainstay of Vidocq's operation. He was
the first to employ women detectives. His list of accomplish-
ments goes on and on.

Many books were published as by Vidocq, although scholars
generally acknowledge they were penned by other writers of the
day. Edwards goes so far as to theorize that *Memoires*, more
fiction than fact, is actually the first detective story, preceding Poe's "Murders in the Rue Morgue" by thirteen years.
But in covering Vidocq's flamboyant lifestyle, Edwards does a
fine job. In some instances where two different stories con-
flict, Edwards relates both. The only problem is that so much
about Vidocq yet today remains mystery. Let us hope as
scholars dig through the archieves more information emerges on
this ingenious personality. (Becky A. Reineke)

E.C.R. Lorac. *Place for a Poisoner*. Doubleday, 1949. First
published as *Part for a Poisoner*. Collins, 1948.

I found this a quietly compelling book. It starts with
the classic situation of an elderly, wealthy man, James Marchent, who falls in love with his nurse, Jean Dellaton, and
announces his intention of marrying her. His two impecunious
nephews, Bill and Dick Marchent, are very upset at this news,
since they are counting heavily on inheriting his fortune.
They consider the nurse to be a conniving opportunist, and
they start to probe her past in an effort to discredit her in
James's eyes. James's housekeeper, Mrs. Transome, is concerned about her future if the marriage does take place. A
brother of James, Matthew Marchent, is a second-rate actor in
poor health; he and his actor friend, Jeremy Jones, are also
expecting money from James's estate.

Into this simmering situation a new charlady, Mrs. Cobbin,
comes to work for Mrs. Transome. On being introduced to the
nurse, Mrs. Cobbin blurts out, "Aren't you nurse Blunt?" Jean
denies this charge, but Bill and Dick follow up this clue with
but little success until a letter from a friend of Mrs. Transome does lead to word about Jean's past. A hint of this gets
to James, who is greatly upset.

In the midst of all this James is found dead, poisoned by
weedkiller. Inspector MacDonald and Sergeant Jenkins start
the investigation by naturally suspecting the nephews. But
things take a non-stereotyped turn when byth Jean and Mrs.
Cobbin disappear. MacDonald and Jenkins unravel the puzzle
by unmasking an ingenious and unsuspected murderer. All the
details are neatly tied up and a satisfactory motive established.
    Very well done, in low-key British Style. (Howard Rapp)

W.R. Burnett. *Goodbye, Chicago*. St. Martin's Press, 1981,
    175 pp., $9.95.

    Nineteen-twenty-nine, the year the stock market crash
permanently altered the shape of American life, was also the
year two extraordinary first novels permanently altered the
landscape of American crime fiction. Dashiell Hammett's *Red
Harvest* and W.R. Burnett's *Little Caesar* swept away earlier
romantic images of the underworld as full of reincarnated
Robin Hoods and sinister hidden masterminds, and replaced them
with portraits of banal, amoral lumps clawing at each other in
the competition to be king of the hill. Hammett's great novels
were written in a sudden spurt, and he published none after
1934, but Burnett proved to be a long-distance runner and continued to turn out both novels (notably *High Sierra* and *The
Asphalt Jungle*) and movie and TV scripts until the late 1960s.
Now at age eighty-one, Burnett is back with a novel of Chicago's police and underworld in 1928, as if by returning to the
time and place of *Little Caesar* he was closing a circle.
    Burnett is famous for his lean, hard style of objective
realism, in which events are described and people talk without
the least trace of emotion, for the simple reason that in the
world of organized crime emotion means weakness and weakness
means you're dead. In *Goodbye, Chicago* the feelings of Burnett's characters are much more in evidence, though still
masked behind clipped dialogue and ritual gestures, and the
conventions of objective realism are broken by the intrusion
more than once of the author's omniscient voice. The novel
begins with the discovery of a woman's body floating in the
river. Whether her death was accident, suicide, or murder is
never made clear, but she was the wife of Detective Sergeant
Joe Rocordi, whom she had deserted three years before in order
to live with the boss of Chicago's houses of prostitution.
Like the circles radiating outward when a stone is dropped in
a pool of water, the events that radiate from the recovery of
Helga Nielsen Ricordi's body shatter the tight-knit underworld
of Chicago just as the stock market crash prepares to shatter
the structure of the world above.
    Burnett in his eighties writes and paces as vigorously as
in the Prohibition Era, and *Goodbye, Chicago* is full of the
kinds of subtle analogies between crime and "legitimate" business, between cops' world and crooks' world, that Burnett and
Hammett in the Twenties all but invented. But the book is so
loosely organized, so routine and unexciting in characterization and incident, so incredibly rich in anachronisms (with
references to Jean Harlow, talking movies, motesl, paperback
books, police radio cars, and slang terms like kook and fink)
that, remembering the dying words of Little Caesar--"Mother

of God, is this the end of Rico?"--one can only hope that this disappointment is not the end of the writing career of W.R. Burnett. (Francis M. Nevins, Jr.)

Richard Lockridge. *The Old Die Young*. Lippencott, 1980.

Lockridge's usual stylistic hang-ups and dialog short-cuts are distracting through the first half of Nathan Shapiro's latest case. New York's theater scene provides the background. Aging star Clive Branson made a smash out of Bret Askew's light comedy *Summer Solstice*. But Branson's sudden death threw some doubt on the continued run of the play. Conscientious police work tracks down the clues that finally unmask the killer. (Fred Dueren)

Gladys Mitchell. *Watson's Choice*. Dell, 1981. First published in 1955.

As one of the most publicized of Gladys Mitchell's books on this side of the Atlantic, *Watson's Choice* came with high credentials, and lived up to those credentials with the English country house setting, red herrings, subplots, and enigmatic hints by Dame Beatrice. A Sherlock Holmes party hosted by Sir Bohun Chantry provides the original impetus for the house party. Sherlockians will enjoy the game in which members of the house party must search for clues mentioned in the first two volumes of Holmes stories. On hand are Sir Bohun's illegitimate son, two young nephews, their governess (soon to be Sir Bohun's fiancee), her would-be lover, and Inspector Gavin, among others. But as delightful as the trappings are, the plot does not sustain them. Dame Beatrice never explains how she knows who the killer is, but merely helps trap him into exposing himself. Lovers of English traditionalism will see this as a book not to be missed; others' enthusiasm will decrease with their preference for action. (Fred Dueren)

Janice Law. *Death Under Par*. Houghton Mifflin, 1981.

Anna Peters' fifth case takes her to England for the British Open. Actually, Harry, her husband, is to go there to do illustrations of the tournament for *Sports Illustrated*, so it seems like a good chance for Anna to take a break from work and enjoy a "working" honeymoon. It doesn't take long for Anna to also be working--the organizers of the Open want her to find out who is vandalizing the course and sending threatening letters to the newest golf star, Peter Bryce. Murder soon follows, and the pace and action are suitably stepped up as the mystery deepens. About halfway through, Anna begins to unfold the complex relationships from Bryce's past. And that is the novel's major flaw. By the time we get to the end, there are no revelations left. A bit of threatening danger and suspense over who wins the Open has to suffice for a finale. Anna is enjoyable and competent, but this time she worked too well, too soon. (Fred Dueren)

Darwin Teilhet. *Hero by Proxy*. Gollancz, 1943.

On the blurb this is described as "a peach of a thriller," but I'm sorry to say that when I'd discovered within thirty pages that it involved World War II spies, that it contained two brothers, one of whom (our hero) is always being mistaken for the other, and that it was set in South America, my interest died completely. A pity, since I've read and enjoyed the Teilhets' earlier Baron von Kaz series. Peach is not my flavour of the month. (Bob Adey)

Ivy Low. *His Master's Voice*. Sampson Low, 1930.

Another little nugget mined from a forgotten thirties seam. It concerns the death, by stabbing, of playboy Arkady Petrovitch Pavlov, and the investigation of the crime by District Procurator Nikolia. Various suspects come in and out of the reckoning--the lovely ballerina, the mysterious dentist, the ballerina's boyfriend--and the criminal is finally caught. But the book's real charm lies in the affectionate picture drawn of pre-war Moscow, and the people who live in it. The description of the street boys (surely the literary descendants of the Baker Street Irregulars) is alone well worth the price of admission.
The book was issued as *Moscow Mystery* by Coward in 1943 and under what I suspect may be the author's real name, Ivy Litvinoff, in a revised edition by Gollancz in 1973. (Bob Adey)

From Becky Reineke, 1648 Zarthan Ave. S., Minneapolis, MN:
    An entire issue of reviews? TMF 5:2 proved murderous to
my reading list. I will never catch up. But I'm thankful for
the insight on books I wouldn't enjoy, which has saved me time
in the long run. Right? ...
    Otto Penzler's letter heartened me considerably. I never
once doubted Otto's affection for mysteries, so perhaps I
should have registered my comments with Brady at CBS. A waste
of time that would have been, I'm sure. Anyone who spends
three hours on just the dollar value of books and won't even
discuss the reasons why people are so interested in them is
beyond hope. I look upon libraries and book shops as others
view churches or temples. When I get to New York City, the
Mysterious Book Shop will be my first stop.

From Barry Van Tilburg, 4380-67th Ave. N., Pinellas Park, FL:
    Loved the letters and reviews in TMF 5:1. The latest
mystery movies I have seen I consider to be pretty good. However, the first two are very gruesome. If you have an extreme
dislike of gore, by all means bypass these movies. The first
is "My Bloody Valentine," another holiday murder spree movie.
The mystery is who is murdering people and why on Valentine's
Day, of all days. It all concerns a local mine and killings
of twenty years ago. It has an air of *Ten Little Indians*
about it. The main characters die one at a time until there
are two left. Who is the murderer? The second is "Maniac,"
in which the mystery is why does he kill. It gives you an insight into the twisted reasoning of a maniac. The third is
the movie "Sphinx," based on the book by Robin Cook. It concerns murder and the smuggling of Egyptian artifacts from an
"undiscovered" tomb. It has the usual chase scenes, fight
scenes, humor, and scenery. Lesley-Anne Down portrays Erica
Baron, an Egyptologist who blunders into a murder and runs
afoul of smugglers. Frank Langella (Dracula) portrays an
official of the Museum of Egyptian Artifacts.
    As for comments by Bob Adey on Dossier #10, I'm not too
sure myself. I wasn't even too sure exactly about the last
book, *Twinkle, Twinkle, Little Spy*. I suppose the only way
to be sure is to ask Mr. Deighton. Guy, according to the new
TV Guide "Nero Wolfe" may be taken off next year. I say
shoot all sponsors. I'm tired of their stupid commercials
anyway. I'd just as soon have pay TV and do away with those

stupid silly commercials. I have received my copy of *Twentieth Century Crime and Mystery Writers*, and I spent most of yesterday and last night looking at it. Much praise to the people who engineered it and to those who contributed to it. Though I can't imagine why the hardback books by Edward S. Aarons about Sam Durrell were left out (a later Dossier).

[*A later letter--*]

I've been trying to catch up on my reading lately. Do you get the series on TV there (it's on PBS down here) called Mystery? They have Dick Francis's Sid Halley on right now. It's pretty good. I hope they show the new British series on Simon Bognor (Dossier #22).

For any of the James Bond Enthusiasts there is a new James Bond book out. It's called *License Renewed* and is written by the famous John Gardner, famous for "Boysie Oakes" (Dossier #13), "Derek Torry" novels, the "Moriarty" journals, and "Big Herbie Kreuger." Bond has picked up a new gun, a Ruger .44 Magnum, and has traded in his Aston Martin for a Saab 900. The book is $9.95 and is published by Richard Marek Publishers.

I am sorry to everyone about the screw-ups on the Nayland Smith dossier. I went by instinct on the dossier. I see even Bob Briney refers to him as Nayland Smith and not Sir Denis Nayland Smith. As for Smith's job, it seems to be obscure. In *The Devil Doctor* he comandeers a car by handing the driver a letter stating his position as a "Burmese Commissioner," which to me means policeman. In *Fu Manchu's Bride* Smith is referred to as "a Chief of some department of Scotland Yard." In *The Mask of Fu Manchu* Smith is referred to as "Assistant Commissioner of Scotland Yard." In the *Trail of Fu Manchu* Smith is referred to as "Ex-Assistant Commissioner of Scotland Yard," called on consultancy basis. He remains the same in other books, helping the FBI (which has a counter-espionage division) and the Secret Service. Inside Doubleday's edition of *Shadow of Fu Manchu* Smith is described as "British Agent and Ex-Scotland Yard Chief." Inside Herbert Jenkins' edition of *Emperor Fu Manchu* Smith is referred to as of the "British Secret Service," as he is also referred to in *The Wrath of Fu Manchu.* I cannot imagine where I got the "Chief Superintendent" bit at. I plead temporary insanity. The associates were a personal observation. Greville and Weymouth were a bit boring to me. As for people who portrayed Smith in the movies I listed the ones I have actually seen. By the way, I never referred to the books as the "Nayland Smith books." Merely as Smith was an agent and Fu Manchu was not. (Bob, you can come and see my books if you wish.) I'll believe anything Bob says about the Collier books, but my edition says:

Copyright, 1931
by Doubleday, Doran & Company, Inc.
Copyright, 1930
by P.F. Collier & Son Company

The McBride bit must have come from Hagan's *Whodunit?* during material search. The same is my only answer to *The Book of Fu Manchu.* Also, as additional information, Smith appears without Fu Manchu in three short stories ("The Blue Monkey," "The Mark of the Monkey," and "The Turkish Yataghan") in other collections of Sax Rohmer short stories, according to the introduction in *The Wrath of Fu Manchu.* Any mistakes were not intentional. Bob's information was interesting and informative.

From Bob Adey, 7 Highcroft Ave., Wordsley, Stourbridge, West
Midlands, DY 8 5LX, England:
    TMF 5:1 was a very good issue with a particularly interest-
ing letter section.
    I also very much appreciated Martin Wooster's comments on
Twentieth Century Crime and Mystery Writers. Most of what
Martin said was very much in need of being said, but I do wonder whether it isn't becoming rather fashionable to knock poor
Robert B. Parker. Am I the only person to have enjoyed *The
Judas Goat*?
    At last I have found a book I liked but Marvin Lachman
didn't. Higgins' *The Digger's Game*. I've enjoyed all the
Higgins I've read, and Eddie Coyle was most effectively and
accurately translated to the big screen with Mitchum ideally
cast as Coyle.
    So to the letter section. Perhaps I can first clear up
the question of the Sherlockian blocks. The story I was referring to--in which Holmes walked several blocks--was written
by an American fan. It grated because we don't refer to
blocks over here--and anyone who's familiar with our ancient
and often chaotic town system will understand why!
    I'm still rather uncertain as to the subject matter and
slant of Jon Breen's book, but that makes it all the more
tantalizing. I have also recently received the Stout bibliography and have to say that it's everything a biblio should
be. My congratulations to all concerned. The one big flaw
is that I couldn't find a single mistake in it, and--damn it,
Guy--you people should know by now that that's all most of us
fans buy bibliographies for. You should have built a few in.
I did in my locked room bibliography! [*I'm certain we did
too. The first time I looked through the finished book I
spotted three errors in a few minutes' time. I've been afraid
to look at it too closely ever since.*]
    Also recently received Skene Melvin's *Crime, Detective,
Espionage, Mystery and Thriller Fiction and Film*, which looks
useful, but only time will tell. Cumbersome title, though.
    As to scholarly articles, who can possibly resist a title
such as "Paradox and Plot in the Novels of Elmer J. Fudd"?
Well, I can, for one.
    New series of Lovesey inspired Sergeant Cribb television
plays over here, this time not, I think, from the books. Last
night's "The Hand That Rocks the Cradle," about royal infants
and anarchist nannies, was competent but unspectacular. [*The
second season of the Sergeant Cribb series began over here a
few weeks back with a ninety-minute rendition of* Waxwork. *I
was surprised to see it, for I remembered reading last year
that Lovesey was working on some original screenplays for the
coming season. Oddly, I found the TV version of* Waxwork *much
better than the book, which is my least favorite Lovesey tale.
Subsequent episodes in the Cribb series have not been based on
extant novels, so far as I can tell.*]

From Jon Breen, 10642 La Bahia Ave., Fountain Valley, CA:
    I haven't read *Crimes Past* by Mary Challis (or any other
Raven House title save one sent me by the author--they haven't
gone on newsstand sale in this area and the publishers don't
seem to want to send review copies), but I have a guess as to
her identity based on clues in Steve Lewis's review. Sara
Woods lives in London, Ontario, has published more than thirty

detective novels, and (like Challis) writes about a lawyer-
detective. Some of her Antony Maitland books are as bad (or
very nearly) as Steve found *Crimes Past*, but others are excellent. She is probably one of the most erratic authors in
the field.

From Rachel Young, 3048 Thompson Ave., Alameda, CA 94501:
Regarding Steve Lewis's question about Mary Challis; could
she be Sara Woods?

From Ev Bleiler, still hiding out somewhere in New Jersey:
You're establishing a bad precedent for the industry. Who
ever heard of a fan mag coming out on time? [*Jeff Meyerson,
for one.*] ...
Lots of interesting letters this issue. I always find
them interesting. Perhaps the debate about scholars, scholarship, academics, etc. will open up a little more. It occurred
to me when reading the Jan/Feb issue that some of your people
confuse scholarship with pedantry. A big difference.
On the various reviews of Reilly's *20th Century*. Neither
of the two reviews that TMF has given Reilly has pointed up
what I think is one of the strongest features of the book;
that is Reilly's share--the brief biogs and the bibliographies.
Reilly has done an incredible job in getting all this information together. I've done similar work myself, and I know how
time consuming it is and how frustrating. If anyone thinks
it's a snap, let him try to dig out biographical information
on a dead third-line writer. This aspect of the book I regard
with awe.
As for individual articles, I suppose one evaluates them
according to one's conception of what the book is supposed to
be and do. (I agree with Bob Aucott that MW is too harsh on
Ms. Hayne.) For me, Reilly is essentially a library reference
work, and I value highest those articles that have some meat
in them. If I approach a new author via Reilly, I would like
to find out things that I cannot get from a blurb or a book
review. For me, polite little appreciations don't have much
value.
Any of your readers have ideas on how one can get review
copies of European foreign language scholarly works on mysteries? I have a stack of dictionaries bouncing up and down,
eager to be used.

From Fred Dueren, 15200 Seminole Dr., Olathe, KS 66062:
I do have a few ... comments on TMF 5:1. Naturally, I
enjoy TMF as much as most of the regular writers. As soon as
it comes I put aside anything else that I'm not already started
on (and sometimes even those) and dig in. I always have my
own comments and ideas I'd like to tell the various contributors, but then when I start to actually write I've forgotten
what I had to say, or it doesn't seem so important. It's only
my opinion. But since most of the stuff in TMF is just others'
opinions, I'm probably safe in throwing mine in too.
Martin Wooster's review of *Twentieth Century Crime and
Mystery Writers*--Martin, did you judge the various reviews and
decide there were some you did not like and then look them up
in the author section to see which ones were by academics? Or
did you scan the bio's of the contributors and then read the
essays by academics to see if you could classify them? It

probably doesn't matter. We all pick and choose the facts and portions of books to prove our points and ignore the rest. But, if they need it, I think it is time that someone gave a little defense to all the scholarly writing and academic interest in mystery fiction. If that interest didn't exist, what state would our fan magazines and availability of information on crime writers be in? (That sentence came out a bit scrambled, but I hope the sense came through.) Stuffiness and stilted writing will cause its own death of interest in what the author has to say. Let's not begin to condemn opinions or styles just because they are presented by an "academic."

Bob Adey asked about reference works referred to most. My current favorite has to be *Twentieth Century Crime and Mystery Writers*. But for just checking titles or dates, I always go to Hubin. For an opinion about an author I go to Symons' *Mortal Consequences*, C. Watson's *Snobbery with Violence*, or *A Catalogue of Crime*. I usually end up also checking in *Encyclopedia of Mystery and Detection*, and *Detectionary*, but they are not my favorites because they tend to be too superficial. I'd like to be able to go more to TAD and TMF and *Poisoned Pen*, but my own records are not clear enough to fully pull out any particular article. Oh, also for checking short story titles I use EQMM 350, Mundell/Rausch's *Detective Shrot Story Bibliography*, and Nieminski's *Saint Magazine Index*.

I guess I'm not really answering the question of which reference works I consider most important, but they have different uses for me.

Finally, on the Nero Wolfe TV series. I thought the first couple of shows were fairly well done. But the farther they went it seemed the farther they got from the traditional little trick of the book. So I have mostly stopped watching. But then I am a reader instead of a watcher, so I tend to always give up a TV program after a few weeks or a month. I'd always rather be reading about a detective than watching it.

From Linda Toole, 147 Somershire Dr., Rochester, NY 14617:

May I come and watch "Nero Wolfe" with you? My family is just about ready to lynch me for the same type of running commentary that has left you companionless--at least during the show. I try to keep quiet, but sometimes it's impossible; the more I see Coote, the more irritated I get.

I'm saddened to find you giving in on the quote-punctuation issue; I'm even sadder that your policy changed in time to be applied to my loc in 5/1. I don't claim perfection for my own grammar, but I feel English needs all the supporters it can get. "If one is going to use a language, one should use it correctly." (CONTEST--The first person to correctly identify the source of the preceding quotation will receive Robert Fish's *The Tricks of the Trade*, hardbound, ex-lib. If there is no correct answer, the most imaginative answer will winn. To spare our Beloved Editor, please send entries to the above address.) No, I am *not* a little old lady English teacher.

On to happier subjects. I can usually expect at least one fascinating (to me) feature per issue. TMF 5/1 has many (and all those wonderful letters) but my favorite is "Hunter and Hunted." Thank you, Jane, for introducing me to Joe Leaphorn and Jim Chee. These books will go straight to the top of my "must read" list. Is Hillerman a Navajo or has he lived on a reservation?

I would be interested in a review of Garfield's version of
Drood. The recent articles in TMF have piques my interest and
I'd like to get a good edition and read it. Any suggestions?

From Mike Nevins, 7045 Cornell, University City, MO   63130:
    In connection with Steve Lewis's review of *Murder Mystery*
by Gene Thompson, I'm certain that Thompson needed no permis-
sion to print a Gerard Manley Hopkins stanza and attribute it
to one of the book's characters, since Hopkins died in 1889
and his works have long been in the public domain. Steve's
right, of course, that this kind of palming off is a dubious
practice anyway.
    The Sweeney Todd — related radio play by John Dickson Carr which
Bob Briney mentioned is "A Razor in Fleet Street," broadcast
in the U.S. on Carr's *Cabin B-13* series and currently available on tape from Steve Lewis.